English Skating

English Skating

Edges and Striking

Principle of Skating Turns

Combined Figure-Skating

By Henry C. Lowther

Edited by B. A. Thurber

Skating History Press

Main text originally published in 1900 (Principle of Skating Turns) and 1902 (Edges and Striking; Combined Figure-Skating).

Introduction and notes © 2019 B. A. Thurber.

All rights reserved.

Author photograph: Henry C. Lowther in 1881. Reproduced by kind permission of the Master and Fellows of Balliol College.

Cover image: Orange by Evan-Amos, courtesy of Wikimedia commons. Modified for this use, which is in accordance with the Creative Commons Attribution-Share Alike 3.0 Unported license:

https://creativecommons.org/licenses/by-sa/3.0/deed.en

Why an orange? English-style skaters used oranges to mark the centers of their combined figures.

ISBN: 978-1-948100-03-8 (b&w paperback)
ISBN: 978-1-948100-04-5 (color hardcover)
LCCN: 2019936930

Skating History Press
Evanston, IL
http://www.skatinghistorypress.com/

Contents

Introduction — 1

English Skating — 3
   English Figure-Skating, by A. E. Crawley . . . 6
   The English style today 12

Sir Henry C. Lowther — 13

This edition — 21

Bibliography — 23

English Skating — 25

Edges and Striking — 27

Preface — 29

Introduction — 31
   Hints for absolute beginners 31

The Edges — 33
   Different directions in which skate can travel . 33
   Explanation of terms outside and inside edge . 34
   Form required in English skating 35
   Summary of essentials of good form 41

Changes of edge or serpentines	42
Importance of using the hips to effect movements in skating	45

Striking — 51
Importance of correct striking	51
General principle of striking	52
Different classes of stroke	53

Special remarks on various classes of stroke — 65
Special remarks on Classes 2 and 3	66
Special remarks on Class 4	71
Special remarks on Class 5	76
Special remarks on Class 6	79

Eights to a centre — 81
Two forwards entire	81
Eights skated with the cross-roll	84

Concluding remarks — 87

Principle of Skating Turns — 91

Movements required in English figure skating — 95
Turns	95
Mohawks and Choctaws	98

Principle of skating turns — 101
Two methods of skating turns	101
Phases of preparation for any turn	104
General remarks	107

Summary of phases of preparation for a turn . 113
Mohawks and Choctaws 118
Special remarks on the different groups of turns 120
Remarks applicable to certain classes of turns
    irrespectively of group to which they be-
    long 127
Hints with regard to special combinations . . 128

Recapitulation   135

Concluding remarks   137

Combined Figure-Skating   141

Preface   143

Combined figure-skating   145
Various styles of combined figure-skating . . . 145
Terms used in combined figure-skating 156
Manner of circling round the centre 161
Imaginary lines and their use 168

Elementary calls   175

Dismiss calls   193

Difficult calls for advanced skaters   195
Set I 196
Set II 198
Set III 200
Set IV 202
Set V 204

Set VI 205
Set VII 208
Set VIII 210
Set IX 212
Set X 214

Appendix I. Hand-in-hand skating — 217
Rules of precedence in side-by-side scuds . . . 217
Side-by-side scuds 218
Face-to-face scuds 220
Scuds as dance steps 223

Appendix II. Care of rinks — 225

Introduction

English Skating

The English style of figure skating flourished around the turn of the last century. It is best remembered for its stiff, upright posture and for the gigantic figures skated by groups. This volume collects three books about figure skating in the English style: *Edges and Striking*, *Principle of Skating Turns*, and *Combined Figure-Skating*. Readers familiar with modern figure skating will find English-style skating strange, but the foundation is the same, and skating in the English style may help their development as skaters because of its emphasis on posture, form, and fundamentals.

Modern figure skating is mainly the descendant of the International, or Continental, style. The English and International styles are distinct, and "[t]o attempt to blend them is to skate both badly."[1] Caroline Creyke[2] compares them directly in her article on skating:

> The difference of style between the best English skaters and those of other nations consists in the absence of all unnecessary movement with the former, and the exaggerated and theatrical attitudes of the latter. The members of the English skating clubs allow no movement of arm or leg which can be avoided. The closer the arms are kept

---

[1] Henry C. Lowther, page 39 in this edition.

[2] Caroline Creyke, "Skating on Artificial Ice," *The Nineteenth Century: A Monthly Review* 41 (1897): 474–486.

to the side and the nearer the legs are to each other, the more finished the skater; and in the English clubs at St. Moritz and other Swiss resorts this rigidity of body and limb is compulsory. But the stiffness and want of grace so often noticeable on members of the English skating clubs are entirely absent from those who have passed their tests in the Engadine,[3] so highly finished is their skating. The French and Swedish skaters who visit our London rinks wave the arms and kick the legs about incessantly in a manner which can be best described as theatrical. In fact there is precisely the same difference between English and foreign skating as there is between dancing in a ball-room and dancing in a ballet. The foreign skaters are perfectly aware of the value of this florid style, and, even if they could skate quietly, they would prefer to attract the multitude by flourishing about their arms and legs; for by so doing they give more effect to the simpler figures, and are able to overcome real difficulties with greater ease.

The best English skaters get no credit from non-skating onlookers, and pass almost unnoticed, because every turn is done with the utmost precision, without a jerk, with-

---

[3] A region of Switzerland where English skaters who could afford it often spent the winter.

out a jump, and with scarcely any movement of the arms and hands; the head and body being perfectly upright, and possibly somewhat stiff in position. No one but a fairly experienced skater can judge of the great difficulty of executing all the most complicated turns in an erect attitude without using the arms for a balancing pole.

I will take the Mohawk as an example of the English and foreign modes of skating the same figure. The Mohawk consists of a curve on the outside edge forward of one foot, and another, almost continuing the same line, on the outside edge backward of the other. Skated in English fashion, the toe of the unemployed foot is dropped just behind the heel of the first foot, in what is called the fifth position in dancing; the body should be erect, and the knees straight. Skated in foreign fashion, the knees are bent throughout the figure. The unemployed foot is waved *in front* of the employed foot, and a little theatrical kick is given with the toe in the air before it is put down on the ice to make the outside backward stroke behind the other. This is both the easiest and the most showy manner of skating the Mohawk, and many people might learn to skate it thus who could never hope to achieve it in the English fashion, especially if they only began figure-skating late in life, as it is a physical impossibility to some people to get their feet one behind the other, toe to heel, when the knees are straight and parallel to one another.

Shortly after Creyke's article appeared, the first of Lowther's three little books, *Principle of Skating Turns*, made it into print. Thirteen years later, the English style had begun to wane. In what was perhaps an attempt to either keep the style alive or eulogize it, A. E. Crawley described it lovingly in an article published in the February 22, 1913 issue of *The Saturday Review*. The following section quotes his article in full.

English Figure-Skating, by A. E. Crawley

It[4] is an insular paradox that figure-skating in the English style is probably the least known of English sports. It is as little likely to pass into the limbo of "sports obsolete" as is the royal game of tennis (which, by the way, I rejoice to see the Prince of Wales is taking up at Oxford), but, like that great game, it is seldom brought before the popular eye. And, during the years 1905 to 1910, when the N.S.A.[5] was unable to hold any competitions, the absence of out-of-doors ice not being counterbalanced by any artificial area sufficiently large—Prince's is too narrow for combined figures—this em-

---

[4]This section was originally published as A. E. Crawley, "English Figure-Skating," *The Saturday Review of Politics, Literature, Science and Art* 116 (February 1913): 235–236.

[5]The National Skating Association, now the National Ice Skating Association, governs figure skating in Great Britain.

inently English art became more than ever secluded and recondite, though at the height of its development in skill.

It was on the huge ice-rinks of S. Moritz and Davos[6] that English skaters created the art out of the elements common to it and to the International style. This was in the 'eighties, and ever since, on an increasing number of Swiss rinks, a "little band" (in Plato's phrase) of English athletes has developed and guarded a unique "craft and mystery". Like Rugby football, with which it has many analogies, as its complement, International skating, has with Association, it has never aimed at popularity, never harboured a professional element, and never hidden its secrets. Of a dozen excellent books on the art the best are by masters in other fields as well, Sir Henry C. Lowther and Mr. E. F. Benson. The former writes of the subtle science of the art like the Platonic Socrates; the latter leads the learner from the premier pas to the final coup de théâtre, like a Dodo turned governess.

The retired paterfamilias, who takes a first-hand interest in the athletic development of his boys or girls, or both, and who takes them out to Switzerland for January, might do worse than study Mr. Benson's charming volume. Of course, there is tobogganing, and of course there is ski-ing; the plank-hoppers just now have a corner and they are deservedly strong; but still there is skating. The other day an Anglo-Indian father asked my advice about skates for his thirteen-year-old daugh-

---

[6]Two resorts in the Engadine. Davos is featured in *The Magic Mountain* by Thomas Mann.

ter. A winter in Switzerland. . . I expounded the difference between English and International skates. This was accepted, as non-essentials always are accepted. I then made the difference essential, and enlarged upon the muscular and athletic polarity of the two styles. Only adult legs can stand the strain of the "continuous movement" which is the capital of the International skater. The only interest he gathers from the swing of arms and body and unemployed leg at a change or turn is continuity. He gathers no speed, and his balance (of all things in all skating this is the super-thing) is a mere reach-me-down, instantaneous and preparatory to another instantaneous spell, the whole business being a pendulum-series, a repetitive switch-back. But the English skater aims at speed and space; his figures are not fifty-inch but fifty-yard movements, and his balance is as permanent as that of an aeroplane. With a few short steps he gets up speed; then, when on his edge—it may be "outside forward" or "inside back", or otherwise—he assumes a position minutely calculated to preserve balance and minimise friction. His skate-blades are relatively low, not stilt-like as are the International's; their edges are parallel, not torpedo-shaped; they are smooth, but not sharp; their curve is of a big radius, six and a half feet. In sympathy with this perfect "carrier", the skater's body observes every principle that conduces to pace and control. The body is upright, the knee rigid, the unemployed leg close to its fellow, the shoulders are sideways, and the head erect. There is no gesticulation, no abandon, no beating of the air. The effect, which to the uninitiated seems so statuesque and possibly wooden, is a nicely calculated tension of bones and muscles, as fixed as a trigger, for purposes of balance, but as full of spring and latent force as a trigger when it is necessary to make a "change" or a "turn" at the orange[7] or elsewhere.

Anyone who has seen a 'Varsity athlete skating a fifty-yard rocker or bracket at full speed can realise the principles of English strength and calm more vividly than in any physical feat. Comparing the movement with the momentary, precarious, and anxious poise of the International doing a turn at his highest speed, one concludes that English skating is athletic, International is terpsichorean. The one is as scientific as motor-driving, the other as emotional as waltzing. As for grace, grace is always "trimmings"; but there is the grace of the knight on his galloping steed, the grace of power in control, and there is the grace of the man on the treadmill, the grace of power in slavery. The perfect poise of the English skater, his terrific but silent speed, his absence of effort combined with the highest potential, his sudden but smooth and bird-like changes of edge—a crucial test of equilibrium and technique—make a combination more expressive of British force and temperament than any athletic movement known. It is a familiar fact that in athletic movements proper woman loses her finality of grace. The reason for this, curiously enough, is the fact that her characteristic

---

[7]Oranges were commonly used to mark the centers of figures. Frances Glover, secretary of the Royal Skating Club, which still practices the English style, notes that the orange's bright color provides a reference point that remains visible even on misty days (Facebook message to editor, March 20, 2019).

movements are English; they are, that is to say, expressive of patience, of force in reserve, not of energy in dissipation. Quite the most beautiful vision of athletic movement I have ever experienced was to see Miss Janet Tooth (one of the only two winners of the diamond figure-skating test[8] of the N.S.A.) skating turns round the ice-rink at Brighton. Tall and fair, with golden hair plaited to her waist, she skated brackets and threes round that rink like one asleep, so perfect was the rhythm and so unconscious the pose. And her speed and strength were those of a man, though she was but sixteen. That was English skating.

On the other hand, I have seen at Manchester ladies, who are exquisite dancers, executing the "school-figures" of the International style. It was a painful sight; not because the ladies skated ill, but because the movements were ipso facto contortionist, as of course they are. The "continuous movement" so-called, by which the skater acquires impetus from a "change" or "turn", is a volun-

---

[8] Kathleen Waldron, "Skating for Ladies," *The Lady's Realm: An Illustrated Monthly Magazine* 5 (1899): 246 notes that the diamond test was introduced in the 1897–1898 season and remarks, "The horrors of this test ... were blissfully welcomed by the skating world, for there existed not a single skater, even among the men, who seemed within measurable distance of passing." It is probably the "Special Ice Figure-Skating Test" appended to list of tests in Montagu S. Monier-Wiliams, *Figure-Skating*, The Isthmian Library 7 (London: A. D. Innes & Co., 1898), 298–292, and is indeed comprehensive. The test requires eight combined figures, ten figures featuring turns with arcs of at least 50 feet, 23 individual figures (including the Maltese cross on all edges and six grapevines), and three creative figures. Passing this test is an incredible accomplishment.

tary destruction of balance made in order to get speed; the body falls forward, so to speak; the foot catches it up; the result of the weight-shifting is an acceleration of momentum. But to engineer this arms and unemployed leg and body-weight have to be exploited in an ensemble of balance, tout à fait acrobatic.

I am not attempting to depreciate the International style; it has its qualities, and no writer can affect them; it has their defects, and no pen can extend them. But its exponents in this country have been for the last year or two somewhat suffragistic; and the average individual who knows nothing about either style (it is not his fault) is liable to be imbued with the prejudice that only one kind of figure-skating exists, the kind that is exploited in dancing-turns on Sundays at Prince's.

As a matter of athletic science, the English style is final where speed, control, and reserve force are called for. In its team-work it is unique and essentially British. A combined figure, skated by one pair against another, round an orange as centre on a rink seventy yards square,[9] is a miracle even to the layman. For even he notes the rhythm of the business and the timing which brings each pair simultaneously to the orange, there to make a difficult rocker or counter and to sail away four-square. The instant after enter the second pair as time-perfect as the first; the whole thing is like the inter-action of two pairs of synchronised tops, spinning in perfect curves to and from a centre and executing reversals of motion en route.

---

[9]Slightly larger than two modern Olympic ice rinks placed side-by-side.

England's winters are a permanent handicap to this noble sport. It has suffered from their apathy, as Rugby football has never had need to, but, believe me, the two sports are brothers. The typical Englishman beneath the Alps or in an English frost (if this accepts the invitation of the N.S.A.) should mark and inwardly digest the character of English skating. He will recognise it at sight by its fruits—an English, strong, unemotional style.

The English style today

Since Crawley wrote in 1913, the English style has gradually disappeared, but a small remnant survives to this date. The members of the Royal Skating Club still practice the English style on summer sessions at the Guildford Spectrum Leisure Centre in England.[10] On their web page, they recommend English-style skating for helping skaters with turns of all types.

The foundations of the English style remain beneath much of modern figure skating. Many coaches still teach their skaters to turn in accordance with Lowther's principle. Lowther's beginner's motto, "Take care of the form and the power will take care of itself"[11] remains good advice.

---

[10] The Royal Skating Club can be found on Facebook and at http://www.theroyalskatingclub.co.uk/.

[11] Page 138 in this edition.

Sir Henry C. Lowther

In his article, A. E. Crawley calls Lowther, the author of the books you are about to read, and his colleague E. F. Benson[12] "masters in other fields as well" as skating. He lets this tantalizing remark stand on its own, without explaining what other fields these men are masters of. E. F. Benson is known for his writing, while Lowther earned his distinction through service to Britain.

Henry Crofton Lowther[13] was born on March 26, 1858, to the Reverend Brabazon Lowther and Ellen Jane Legh.[14] Little is known about Lowther's father,

---

[12] Author of *English Figure Skating: A Guide to the Theory and Practice of Skating in the English Style* (London: G. Bell & Sons, 1908) and numerous works of fiction.

[13] James R. Hines, *The English Style: Figure Skating's Oldest Tradition* (Westwood, MA: Neponset River Press, 2008), 13, 102 calls the author "Henry Cecil Lowther," which is the name of another man who lived around the same time. Credit is due to Elaine Hooper of the National Ice Skating Association and Frances Glover of the Royal Skating Club for finding the correct Henry C. Lowther. Hooper based her identification on the different knighthoods the two men received and two addresses in the NISA's membership records (emails to editor, March 7 and 8, 2019). Glover found "Sir Henry Crofton Lowther" listed in the records of the Royal Skating Club (email to editor, March 23, 2019). I have written more about the two Henry C. Lowthers in "The Two Henry C. Lowthers," *Pagophilia* (blog), March 26, 2019, https://pagophilia.com/2019/03/26/the-two-henry-c-lowthers/.

[14] *Who Was Who 1929–1940* (London: Adam & Charles Black, 1941), s.v. "Lowther, Sir Henry Crofton."

but his mother is a historical curiosity. She was the only child of Ellen Turner and Thomas Legh.[15] Ellen Turner's brief life revolved around a headline-worthy scandal. When she was only 15, she was abducted and forced to marry Edward Gibbon Wakefield. Fortunately, her family tracked her down and rescued her. They got the marriage annulled and, two years later, she married Thomas Legh. When she was 19, she died in childbirth.[16]

Ellen Jane Legh, Lowther's mother, was raised by her father. When she was 13 years old, her father married Maud Lowther. Maud's last name is no coincidence: our Lowther's father, Brabazon, was her brother. He and Ellen Jane married when he was 33 and she was just 17—the same age her mother had been when she married. It was a good match for him, but not

---

[15]"Memorial page for Ellen Turner Legh (12 Feb 1811–17 Jan 1831)." Find A Grave Memorial no. 192280576. St. Oswald Churchyard, Winwick, Warrington Unitary Authority, Cheshire, England. Maintained by Peter H. (contributor 47423563). In *Find A Grave* database and images, https://www.findagrave.com/.

[16]Details of the lurid story surrounding Turner's abduction can be found in Kate M. Atkinson, *Abduction: The Story of Ellen Turner* (Stockport: Blenkins, 2002) and Abby Ashby and Audrey Jones, *The Shrigley Abduction: A Tale of Anguish, Deceit and Violation of the Domestic Hearth* (Stroud: Sutton Publishing, Ltd., 2003).

so great for her. Ellen Jane supplied the family fortune by inheriting the Shrigley estate when her grandfather died in 1842 and, in 1857, £20,000 from her father.[17]

Our Lowther lived in Pott Shrigley as a child.[18] The 1861 census entry for his household includes, in addition to three-year-old Henry Cecil, his parents; older siblings Brabazon (age 13), William (age 11), and Constance (age 5); three visitors; and thirteen servants (ten women and three men). The Cheshire Parish Registers also record the brief lives of sisters Ellen Rosalie (christened on February 4, 1852 and buried on May 9, 1853)[19] and Sophia (christened on October 23, 1853, and buried just two days later).[20]

---

[17] Abby Ashby and Audrey Jones, *The Shrigley Abduction: A Tale of Anguish, Deceit and Violation of the Domestic Hearth* (Stroud: Sutton Publishing, Ltd., 2003), 189–90.

[18] "1861 England and Wales Census." Henry Lowther in household of Brabaron Lowther, Pott Shrigley, Cheshire, England. PRO RG 9, The National Archives, Kew, Surrey. Found on FamilySearch (https://familysearch.org/ark:/61903/1:1:M7VQ-MZQ; December 8, 2017).

[19] "England, Cheshire Parish Registers, 1538–2000." Ellen Rosalie Lowther, February 4, 1852, Christening: item 6, p. 193, and May 9, 1853, Burial: item 11, p. 82. Pott Shrigley, Cheshire, England, Record Office, Chester; FHL microfilm 2,105,376. Found on FamilySearch (https://familysearch.org/ark:/61903/1:1:F355-FJF; 12 February 2018).

[20] "England, Cheshire Parish Registers, 1538-2000." Sophia Lowther, October 23, 1853, Christening: item 6, p. 203, and October 25, 1853, Burial: item 11, p. 83. Pott Shrigley, Cheshire, England, Record Office, Chester, FHL microfilm 2,105,376. Found on FamilySearch (https://familysearch.org/ark:/61903/1:1:F355-N85; February 12, 2018).

Lowther was educated at Harrow[21] and Balliol College, Oxford, where he enrolled in 1877. He studied modern history and received his BA in 1881 and his MA in 1887. His BA was fourth class—the lowest passing grade—which suggests that he was a rather poor student. Athletics may have distracted him from his studies. He was a member of the rowing team and captain in 1881.[22] He may also have learned to skate in Oxford. The Oxford University Skating Club was founded in 1880,[23] while Lowther was there.

In 1883, Lowther joined the Diplomatic Service traveled the world. He was assigned to The Hague, Stockholm, Berlin, Rio de Janeiro, Constantinople, Madrid, and Bern during the 1880s and 1890s.[24] In 1899, Lowther joined the National Skating Association and the Davos Skating Club.[25] He was clearly not a beginner, because he passed the three English-style skating tests that year—third class on February 11, then second and first class on March 18. There is no record of him attempting the special diamond test; instead, he began

---

[21]The Harrow School is an all-boys boarding school in London that still exists today; information can be found at https://www.harrowschool.org.uk/.

[22]Ivo Elliott, ed., *The Balliol College Register: 1833–1933*, 2nd ed. (Oxford: Oxford University Press, 1934), 98.

[23]Montagu S. Monier-Williams, Winter Randell Pidgeon, and Arthur Dryden, *Figure Skating, Simple and Combined* (London: Macmillan & Co., 1892), 165.

[24]Elliott, *The Balliol College Register: 1833–1933*, 98.

[25]Information about Lowther's skating comes from the records of the National Ice Skating Association, Nottingham, UK, and was graciously provided by Elaine Hooper, the Association's historian.

English Skating

Lowther's rowing team at Head of the River in 1879. Left to right: W. H. P. Rowe, E. A. Upcott, J. Twigg, M. R. Portal, H. C. Lowther, A. A. Wickens, Sir S. B. Crossley, W. A. B. Musgrave, and B. W. Randolph. Reproduced by kind permission of the Master and Fellows of Balliol College.

judging. Within a year, he was on the first class panel. In 1900, he judged in Grindelwald for the whole season, January through March, and published his first book, *Principle of Skating Turns*. Two years later, *Edges and Striking* and *Combined Figure-Skating* appeared.

The books may have been Lowther's way of staying in touch with the skating world while he was abroad. In 1901, he became the Secretary of Legation in Rio de Janeiro, and in 1906, he became the Councillor of Embassy in Tokyo.[26] This year was a turning point in Lowther's life. He married Dorothy Olga St. John on July 19, 1906,[27] and the two promptly departed for New York, arriving on August 4.[28] They had two children, Oliver Peter Lowther (1910–1990) and Esmée Katalin Lowther (1913–1992)[29]

It is difficult to track Lowther's skating through these years because of spotty records. The NISA records that he judged in Switzerland during January in 1908 and 1912, but not in the other months of the season. Perhaps his work kept him from staying longer; he was the Minister to Chile from 1909 to 1912. In

---

[26] Elliott, *The Balliol College Register: 1833–1933*, 98.

[27] Darryl Lundy, *The Peerage: A Genealogical Survey of the Peerage of Britain as well as the Royal Families of Europe*, 2019, s.v. "Sir Henry Crofton Lowther." http://www.thepeerage.com/.

[28] "New York, Passenger and Crew Lists (including Castle Garden and Ellis Island), 1820-1957." Henry C. Lowther, 1906. Found on FamilySearch (https://familysearch.org/ark:/61903/1:1:JF8H-PMG; January 30, 2018).

[29] Lundy, *The Peerage: A Genealogical Survey of the Peerage of Britain as well as the Royal Families of Europe*, s.v. "Sir Henry Crofton Lowther."

1912, he became the Minister at Copenhagen,[30] and in 1913 and 1914, he received two different knighthoods: first KCMG, then GCVO.[31] KCMG is the rank of Knight Commander in the Order of Saint Michael and Saint George. Members of the Order have served Britain in other countries; ambassadors, like Lowther, were appointed frequently. Lowther's second knighthood, GCVO, is perhaps more interesting. Members of the Royal Victorian Order have served the monarch's family personally. Lowther received the Grand Cross, which is the highest honor in this Order. He also received the Grand Cross of the Order of the Dannebrog in Denmark,[32] which is awarded for civil service, in keeping with his diplomatic role.

In 1916, Lowther retired from diplomatic work. After a short break, he returned to skating. The Royal Skating Club's minute book notes that "Sir Henry Crofton Lowther was re-elected a Subscriber & Member, having paid an amount equal to the subscriptions for the present and past seasons" on January 4, 1918. Once he had been reinstated, the Royal Skating Club's membership lists record that he was elected to the committee of the Skating Club in 1919 and re-elected in 1928.[33] There is no record that he ever won a competition, but he clearly knew his skating well and valued his involvement in the sport.

---

[30]Elliott, *The Balliol College Register: 1833–1933*, 98.

[31]Anonymous, "Sir Henry Lowther: Former Minister in Copenhagen," *The Times* (London), November 27, 1939, 8.

[32]Ibid.

[33]Frances Glover, email to editor, March 23, 2019.

On November 23, 1939, Lowther passed away at his home on Sittingbourne Road, Maidstone, Kent.[34] He was 81 years old.

---

[34] Anonymous, "Sir Henry Lowther: Former Minister in Copenhagen."

This edition

This edition is based on the copies of the three books in my collection. It includes all the original text, but I have taken some liberties with the organization of section and chapter headings and with the presentation of tables and diagrams. I have also standardized the spelling of Choctaw (not Chocktaw, which Lowther occasionally used) and silently corrected other obvious errors. Furthermore, I added the images on pages 37 and 145 and all the footnotes.

I am grateful to Elaine Hooper of the National Ice Skating Association, Frances Glover of the Royal Skating Club, the reference librarians at the Evanston Public Library and the Newberry Library, the Special Collections Department of the Bodleian Library at Oxford University, and the Balliol College Archive for help finding biographical information on Lowther.

Bibliography

Anonymous. "Sir Henry Lowther: Former Minister in Copenhagen." *The Times* (London), November 27, 1939, 8.

Ashby, Abby, and Audrey Jones. *The Shrigley Abduction: A Tale of Anguish, Deceit and Violation of the Domestic Hearth.* Stroud: Sutton Publishing, Ltd., 2003.

Atkinson, Kate M. *Abduction: The Story of Ellen Turner.* Stockport: Blenkins, 2002.

Benson, E. F. *English Figure Skating: A Guide to the Theory and Practice of Skating in the English Style.* London: G. Bell & Sons, 1908.

Crawley, A. E. "English Figure-Skating." *The Saturday Review of Politics, Literature, Science and Art* 116 (February 1913): 235–236.

Creyke, Caroline. "Skating on Artificial Ice." *The Nineteenth Century: A Monthly Review* 41 (1897): 474–486.

Elliott, Ivo, ed. *The Balliol College Register: 1833–1933.* 2nd ed. Oxford: Oxford University Press, 1934.

Hines, James R. *The English Style: Figure Skating's Oldest Tradition.* Westwood, MA: Neponset River Press, 2008.

Lundy, Darryl. *The Peerage: A Genealogical Survey of the Peerage of Britain as well as the Royal Families of Europe*, 2019. http://www.thepeerage.com/.

Monier-Wiliams, Montagu S. *Figure-Skating*. The Isthmian Library 7. London: A. D. Innes & Co., 1898.

Monier-Williams, Montagu S., Winter Randell Pidgeon, and Arthur Dryden. *Figure Skating, Simple and Combined*. London: Macmillan & Co., 1892.

Thurber, Bev. "The Two Henry C. Lowthers." *Pagophilia* (blog), March 26, 2019. https://pagophilia.com/2019/03/26/the-two-henry-c-lowthers/.

Vandervell, H. E., and T. Maxwell Witham. *A System of Figure-Skating: Being the Theory and Practice of the Art as Developed in England, with a Glance at Its Origin and History*. 1st ed. London: Macmillan & Co., 1869.

Waldron, Kathleen. "Skating for Ladies." *The Lady's Realm: An Illustrated Monthly Magazine* 5 (1899): 245–250.

Who Was Who 1929–1940. London: Adam & Charles Black, 1941.

English Skating

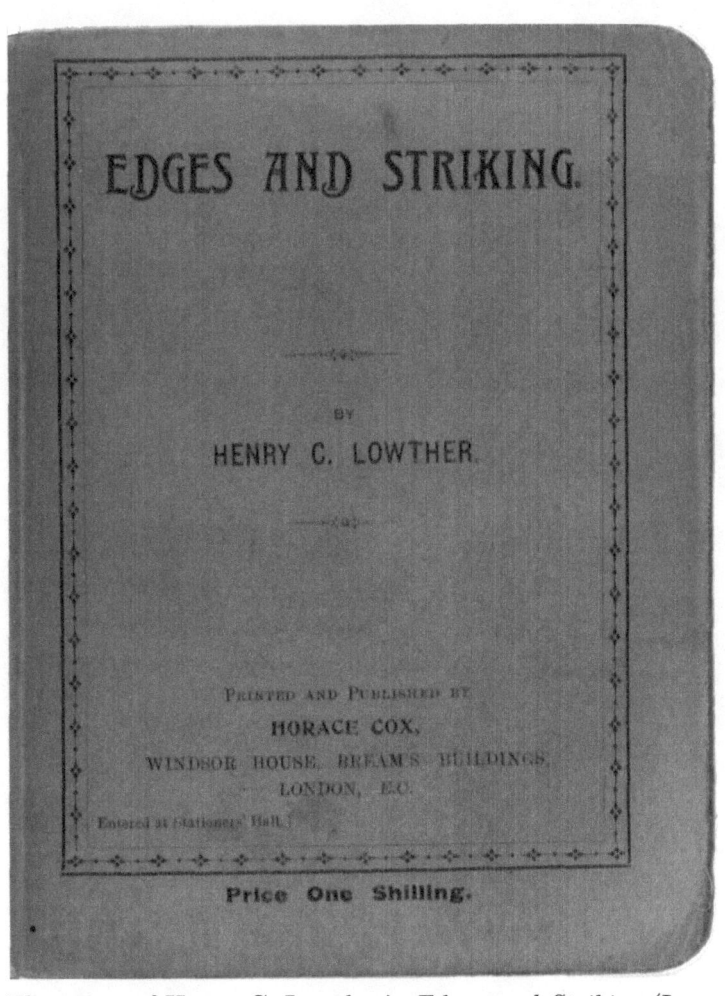

The cover of Henry C. Lowther's *Edges and Striking* (London: Horace Cox, 1902).

Preface

The movements required for English figure-skating are strictly limited. The apprenticeship required to become an efficient performer in the purely English style necessitates merely a thorough acquaintance with the four edges, both simple and in combination in the form of a serpentine; efficiency in the correct manner of taking up a fresh stroke, that is, in launching on to the required edge; and, lastly, facility, while travelling on any given edge, in preparing for, and executing, any one of the four turns which it is possible for the skate to make while on that edge.

The whole range of English skating may therefore be comprised under the three headings "Edges," "Striking," and "Principle of Skating Turns," and the subject is dealt with in this simplified manner.

The present treatise deals with the subject of "Edges" and "Striking."

Having acquired proficiency in these three elements of which English skating consists, the skater is ready to learn the principles of "combined figure-skating," which is the *raison d'être* of the English style, and for which these two treatises are intended as a preparation.

Some apology would appear necessary for the publication of anything fresh on a subject which has been already so ably handled by more than one competent expert. That apology may be found, as regards the present treatise, in the conspicuous absence of anything like a studied system of striking among a considerable class of skaters, who, but for this radical defect, might reach a higher standard, and whose attention it is hoped may be arrested by the prominence here given to this elementary, though wholly indispensable, acquirement.

HENRY C. LOWTHER

Introduction

Beginners who have never had on skates must be in a position to skate freely about the ice with a certain amount of confidence, without troubling themselves about edges and other technicalities, before studying the following chapters on "Edges" and "Striking."

Hints for absolute beginners

Motion of skating has nothing in common with that of walking

The only practical hint to absolute beginners is to point out that skating has nothing in common with the motion of walking. In walking one foot is swung forward and placed on the ground in advance of the body, and at some distance from the other, the leg being straight, and the weight being gradually transferred from one leg to the other. In skating this is impossible.

Method of progression in skating consists of standing on one foot and pushing with the other

The foot must be placed on the ice close to the other, with the knee bent, immediately under the skater, so that he can stand on it with his whole weight; while propulsion is obtained by a vigorous thrust with the other leg, the foot of which then leaves the ice. Once under way the skater must gradually draw himself up and travel with a straight leg till the next stroke is taken, when the operation is repeated, the feet changing *rôles*.

Correct position of feet when taking a forward stroke

Care must be taken to place the skate on the ice with the heel in the hollow of the other foot, and at an angle of about 45° to it, in order that the propelling foot may obtain a firm purchase with the inside of the blade for the thrust. Thus:

Left foot.

Right foot (propelling foot).

Further hints useless till the beginner can move freely about the ice

Having grasped the idea that it is impossible to walk on a slippery surface with skates on, as on dry land, and having learnt to propel himself in the manner described, first travelling on one leg, then on the other, the beginner will soon be able to move freely about the ice. As soon as he has reached this point, he is in a position to begin to learn to skate, and should at once pursue the chapters on "Edges" and "Striking," which must be studied concurrently.

The Edges

Different directions in which skate can travel

The skate is capable of travelling in three directions, both forwards and backwards.

1. In a straight line, to do which it must be on the flat of the blade.

2. On a curve to the right, by leaning over to the right. And

3. On a curve to the left, by leaning over to the left.

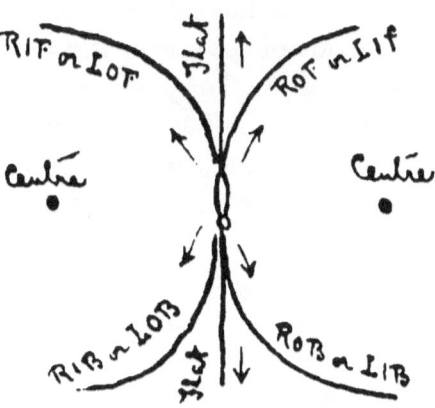

Diagram illustrating different directions in which skate can travel.

N.B.—The following abbreviations are used throughout:
  R O F = Right foot, outside forward.
  R I F = Right foot, inside forward.
  R O B = Right foot, outside back.
  R I B = Right foot, inside back.
  L O F = Left foot, outside forward.
  L I F = Left foot, inside forward.
  L O B = Left foot, outside back.
  L I B = Left foot, inside back.

Explanation of terms outside and inside edge

These right and left curves are identical in nature, though one is called a curve of outside, the other of inside, edge, according to which foot it is skated on.

The expressions "outside" and "inside" edge are purely arbitrary, and adopted merely as distinctive terms to indicate the direction of the curve. If on the right foot, the outside edge carries the skater on a curve to the right; and the inside on a curve to the left, the converse being the case for the left foot.

The nature of the movement of the skate, however, is in both cases identical, since to whichever side it leans it travels on a curve inclining towards the centre of the circle of which this curve is a portion of the circumference, and is therefore, correctly speaking, always on the inside edge. The terms outside and inside edge are not therefore properly applicable to the skate, but rather to the skater's foot. When on the right foot, he has to lean over on the outside of the foot to skate any portion of the circumference of a circle, the centre of which is on his right hand, and is hence said to be travelling on the outside edge; whereas, he leans over on the inside of the right foot to skate any portion of the circumference of a circle, the centre of which is on his left hand, and is therefore said to be travelling on the inside edge.

The terms outside and inside edge as applied to the skate are, however, established by custom, and it is better to preserve them as being readily understood, though not strictly speaking correct.

Form required in English skating

The following will explain to the beginner the essential features of good form, according to the English style.

Theoretical ideal attitude for all edges, completely sideways

Theoretically, the ideal attitude for all edges is completely sideways, the shoulders, hips, and travelling foot being in the same straight line, with the head turned towards the direction of progress, forward, if travelling forward, back, if travelling backwards, and never looking down at the feet. The unemployed leg should hang loosely and easily behind the other, with the feet close together, their exact relative position slightly varying according to the natural balance of the skater; while the arms should remain in a perfectly natural, easy position, close to the body. The one on the same side as the employed leg may be bent at the elbow, and the forearm carried across the body, should this attitude come naturally to the skater, but the other should hang loosely down with the elbow turned in—that is, thumb outwards.

In this attitude, if the body is vertical, the skater is travelling on the flat of the skate; whereas, by a slight inclination to one side or the other, he is at once travelling on whichever edge he desires, the position of the head alone being different in forward and back edges.

Modification of ideal attitude necessary

Now this ideal attitude is an exaggeration of what is possible in practice, since it would necessitate a strained position. It must therefore be modified, the skater merely travelling as sideways as he conveniently can, consistently with a perfectly easy carriage.

Correct carriage

The employed leg while travelling on any edge must be perfectly *straight and braced*, and the body perfectly *upright*, with the chest thrown out, though avoiding anything like stiffness.

Stiffness to be avoided

It cannot be too strongly impressed on the beginner that, *with the exception of the employed leg*, everything must be loose and easy, though in form and thoroughly

The correct posture for a forward inside edge in English-style skating, according to H. E. Vandervell and T. Maxwell Witham, *A System of Figure-Skating: Being the Theory and Practice of the Art as Developed in England, with a Glance at Its Origin and History*, 1st ed. (London: Macmillan & Co., 1869), plate 1.

under control. There can be no delicate sense of balance where there is rigidity, which, moreover, has a tendency to set up friction.

Reasons for skating with a straight leg, in the English style

The straight employed leg and upright carriage of the body are necessary features of the English style, on practical, if not on æsthetic grounds. To those only familiar with the Continental style, this gives an appearance of stiffness, but it is the only style compatible with the speed and size of the movements exclusively skated, and which demand a light edge throughout. It is the question of pace, which is of importance in English skating alone, that renders the style adopted necessary. Any skater can easily convince himself, by experiment, that, with a permanently bent knee, there is a tendency to get on too hard an edge, that his speed diminishes, and that no impetus is acquired on making a turn. Size and pace being essential features of first class English skating, a bent knee must therefore be regarded as a radical fault, no less than a rigidly straight leg in continuous skating, where the movement is facilitated by the contrary. It is not therefore merely for the sake of uniformity in combined figure-skating that a particular attitude is prescribed.

It may be argued that in speed-skating the knee is bent; but in speed-skating a simple edge alone is required and not a series of evolutions. It is in skating the latter that a bent knee results in too hard an edge.

The vexed question of the straight as opposed to the

bent leg, which has been freely discussed by partisans of the different styles, need not leave any doubt on the skater's mind as to which is right. Both are right, but on different occasions. One class of movements requires a straight, the other a bent, leg, and the two styles should be kept perfectly distinct. To attempt to blend them is to skate both badly.

Skater should travel on back part of skate

If travelling in the correct attitude, the skater will be on the back part of the skate nor will an erect position admit of the weight being permanently further forward than over the very centre of the blade, a temporary easing off of the weight so as to get momentarily on the front part of the skate, when desired, alone being possible without leaning forward.

Importance of upright carriage

It is impossible to exaggerate the importance of standing upright when skating in the English style. The failure to do so is, in nine cases out of ten, the cause of any difficulty experienced in executing a movement.

Position of the unemployed foot

As to the exact position of the unemployed foot when travelling on any edge, no hard-and-fast rule can be laid down, except that the feet should be close together, since the proper position, provided this requirement be fulfilled, is that which is best suited to the natural balance of the skater. One person may require to keep the feet heel to heel; another to carry the unemployed foot slightly further behind, in order to obtain a correct balance, and only experience can teach the exact position required in each individual case. The sinking of the heel and turning up of the toe of the unemployed foot, which is advocated by some, cannot be recommended on æsthetic grounds, and it is doubtful whether this attitude can claim any real advantage to justify its ugliness.

Body must prepare beforehand for requirements of succeeding edge

The above is sufficient to explain to beginners the nature of and correct attitude for the four edges. It must, however, be clearly understood that the body must be prepared *beforehand* for this attitude, that is, while still travelling on one foot, the skater must, before putting down the other, begin to reverse the semi-sideways attitude with one shoulder leading, for a semi-sideways attitude with the other shoulder leading, the stroke being taken during this process, which is finally completed on launching on to the new edge. A corresponding change must of course be made in the position of the head, the whole process being smooth and deliberate.

Effected by shifting the arms

This change in the position of the shoulders, which, as stated, must be made before the change of foot, is effected by pressing back to arm corresponding to the employed leg, while the other arm is brought slightly across the body, this being their correct carriage for the new edge.

In all movements, it may be remarked, necessitating a reversal of the arms, *without* a change of foot, the arms having performed their functions revert to their original position, since their correct permanent position is always the same as long as the skater travels on the same leg. Any alteration in their position is therefore merely temporary, requiring a counter-movement to bring them again into the correct attitude.

Summary of essentials of good form

Such, then, are the essentials of good form, in the English style, when travelling on any edge, which cannot be better summarised than they have already been in more than one work on skating, as follows, namely:

1. Semi-sideways attitude of the body.

2. Face turned in the direction of progress.

3. Uprightness of carriage.

4. Straightness of the employed leg.

5. Approximation of the feet.

The beginner has only to consider how far his attitude fulfils these conditions to know for himself what he has to correct.

Changes of edge or serpentines

While travelling on any curve a change of edge may be effected, producing a figure in the shape of the letter **S**, or an inverted S, thus—**Ƨ**. This movement is known as a serpentine.

How to skate

In all changes of edge the skate has necessarily to pass over the flat of the blade, and the body consequently to come up to the vertical during the process, which is facilitated by accentuating the curve with the foot, just before the change, more than is compatible with the inclination of the body. This swerving away from the direction ultimately aimed at must be sufficient not only to bring the body up to the perpendicular, but to make it slightly overbalance in the other direction. The alteration in the direction of the curve which the skater is then compelled to make to recover his balance, by bringing the foot more under him, changes the edge, and equilibrium is restored.

This is effected principally by hip-play, the hip of the unemployed leg coming momentarily forward just before the change, and then going back again, in forward changes of edge, while in back changes of edge it is momentarily forced back previous to the change, and then allowed to come forward again.

The following diagram illustrates the effect of the accentuation of the curve, causing it to deviate from the direction it would otherwise take. The inclination of the body meanwhile remains as required for a true balance on the curve, shown by the dotted line, from which the foot swerves.

Change of edge from O F to I F

In changing from O F to I F, it is of assistance to look back for a moment over the shoulder corresponding to the unemployed leg at the change of edge.

Change of edge from I B to O B

In changing from I B to O B, likewise, turning round the head for a moment away from the direction of progress—that is, looking over the shoulder corresponding to the employed leg—facilitates the change.

Rules as to position of the head not to be too slavishly adhered to

The general rules as to the proper position of the head for each edge must not be too slavishly adhered to. Such rules are merely intended to facilitate the movement, and when a slight deviation from them is found better to serve this end, their too strict observance would defeat the very subject they have in view.

Semi-sideways attitude of body differs on different edges

It will be found in practice that, when travelling on the outside forward edge, the body is less sideways than on the inside forward edge, the converse being the case for the back edges, it always being assumed that the sideways attitude adopted is such as prescribed, namely, the limit consistent with an easy carriage.

Result as regards serpentines

It follows from this that, when skating serpentines, in changing from O F to I F, and from I B to O B, the shoulders must be brought more into line with the travelling foot, in order to be in the correct position for the new edge—that is, a more sideways attitude must be adopted. The converse is naturally the case for the other changes of edge, namely, I F to O F, and O B to I B.

Part of skate on which changes of edge should be made

Forward changes of edge should be made on the heel; back changes of edge more on the front part of the skate.

Importance of using the hips to effect movements in skating

While travelling on any edge, the hips and shoulders should be in the same straight line, and no movement can be made with the hips without the effect being felt. The mobility of the hips, which can be twisted in either direction independently of the shoulders and arms, enables the skater to utilise this knowledge, and gives him an immense reserve fund of power, by judicious application of which he can effect and control any movement with the minimum of shoulder and arm work. The arms are useful auxiliaries, but it is on the play of the hips that the skater should chiefly depend. This is the secret of quiet skating, and the absence of all apparent effort, by which alone a standard suggestive of the motto "ars est celare artem"[35] can be realised.

How to practice edges and how to check rotation

In practising edges care should be taken to give the same value to each curve, and to be fairly light on the edge, since the tendency of the beginner is always to err in the other direction, which often entails loss of control over the movement.

Should rotation be set up by getting too hard on the edge, the remedy, in order to check it, and recover control over the movement, is as follows: If travelling on the O F or I B edge, the sideways attitude should be increased by getting the shoulders more in a line with

---

[35]"It is art to conceal art."

the employed foot; while, if travelling on the I F or O B edge, a less sideways position should be adopted by bringing the shoulders approximately at right angles to the employed foot. This should be effected slowly and smoothly, and as soon as control is regained the correct attitude for the edge should again be assumed.

This is better than incurring the risk of being involuntarily whipped round by the skate, which is in a possible contingency when rotation has been set up, though where a rectification is necessary the movement cannot be regarded as otherwise than faulty. The method of bringing the body up to the vertical made use of in changing the edge when skating serpentines affords the skater another, and equally powerful, corrective, but involves momentarily accentuating still more the curve which is already too pronounced.

The best way to acquire the habit of making curves of a uniform size is to skate them alternately on the opposite sides of an imaginary straight line. Thus:

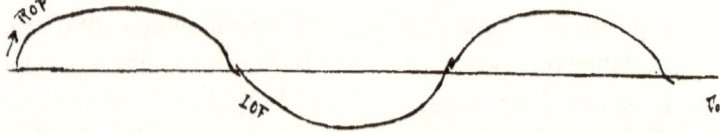

To do this, the skater should note some landmark towards which he must progress by means of curves, first in one direction, then in the other.

Striking off with the travelling foot approximately at right angles to the imaginary line down which he has to make his way, he travels on the same foot till the curve brings him back to it, but facing in the opposite direction.

He then strikes off with the other foot approximately at right angles to the imaginary line, and so on. If the stroke is taken exactly at right angles to the imaginary line, and a true edge maintained throughout, complete semicircles will be skated; if at an angle less than a right angle, smaller segments of a circle will be skated.

How to practice serpentines

Similarly in practising serpentines, use may be made of an imaginary straight line, the change of edge occurring when the first curve brings the skater back to it. Thus—

If it is desired to continue along the same line with a serpentine on the other foot, the other edge must be skated first.

Counting up to the same number at a uniform pace, on either foot, is another method of ensuring uniformity in the size of the curves skated, if the same strength of stroke is obtained each time.

Correct manner of striking essential

To put this into practice necessitates, however, a knowledge of the correct manner of taking up a stroke; indeed, the subject of edges is inseparably connected with that of striking, since, in order to skate any edge properly, the skater must know how to launch himself on to it in the correct manner.

Chapter II., on striking, should therefore be carefully perused concurrently with the preliminary chapter on edges, since in treating of striking it necessarily treats of edges as well. Either chapter may be regarded as the complement of the other, and the two together contain all the elementary instruction necessary previous to studying the principle of skating turns.

English Skating

Striking

Summary of different classes of strokes showing positions of feet when striking

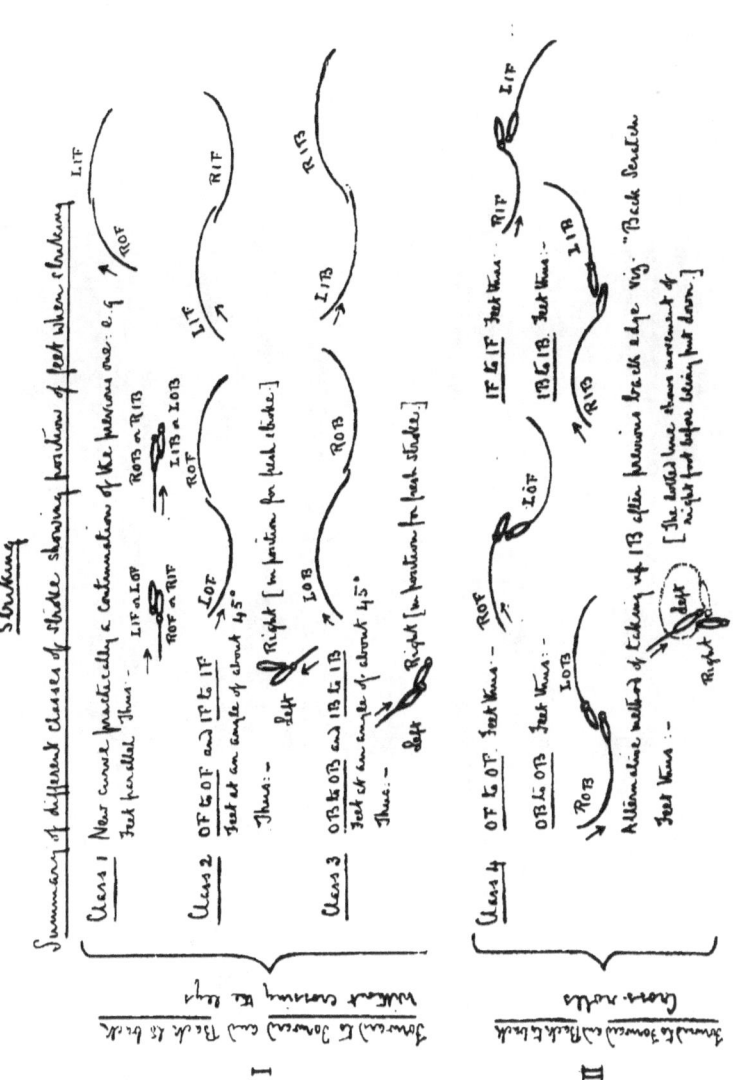

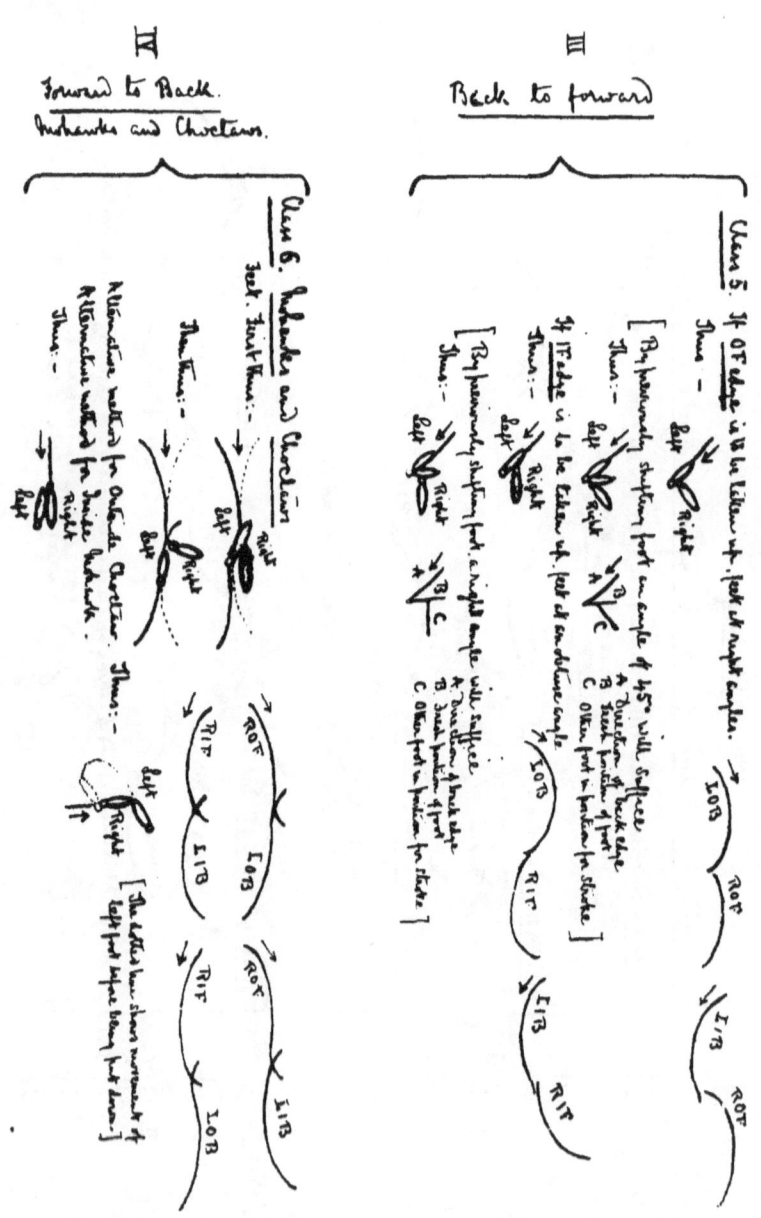

Striking

The foregoing Tables show the different classes of stroke and the position of the feet when striking.

These strokes will be discussed in detail further on.

Importance of correct striking

Correct striking, that is taking up a fresh stroke from one foot to the other, is the basis of all good skating, an acquirement too often neglected in the haste to get on to something more interesting. A longer apprenticeship, however, in this elementary branch would amply repay any trouble taken, since only by accurate striking can the skater acquire power without visible effort, and be perfectly steady with a correct balance the moment he launches on to an edge, without which the subsequent movement cannot be satisfactorily skated. This subject therefore claims special attention, and is here dealt with at some length, in view of the fact that the large majority of skaters attach little or no importance to the exact relative position of the feet when taking a stroke, thereby losing a considerable part of the power to be obtained from the thrust, or push, with the leg about to leave the ice.

Correct striking is, however, the secret of power and a perfectly steady balance, and the key to sound, steady skating.

General principle of striking

The general principle of striking is as follows:

When taking a fresh stroke *forwards*, the knees must be bent as the foot is put down *firmly on the heel*, almost touching, and at an angle to, the other, while the body must swing fell down over the knee for the stroke, which consists of a vigorous thrust from the foot about to leave the ice.

In ordinary plain strokes (*i.e.*, without crossing the legs), the push, or thrust, is from the inside of the blade, the skate, if not already on that edge, rolling over to admit of this; and the thrust should commence with the back part of the skate, and extend along the blade, till finally the toe leaves the ice. Beginners are specially cautioned against obtaining the stroke from the toe alone, the business part of the thrust being, rather, from the *back* part of the skate.

This thrust with the leg is the principle motive power, but additional momentum may be obtained by utilising properly the swing of the body. This is effected by drawing the body up to its full height, till it slightly rocks back, just before the foot is placed on the ice, whereby increased power is acquired for swinging forward the weight loosely and smoothly on to the new curve. As the body swings forward and the knees bend, all the muscles should be relaxed, the moment being one of complete repose. The motive power, then, consists of two factors, the thrust with the leg, and body swing, the latter being almost as important as the former, since without it the skater cannot use his weight to advantage.

Finally, when the stroke is obtained, the body is slowly drawn up, the leg straightened, and the heels brought together without any jerk.

In taking a stroke *backwards*, the movement is analogous, but body swing is only possible in a modified degree. In back strokes the weight should *not* be planted firmly on the heel at once, as in forward strokes, but should be gradually shifted back, while travelling.

This is the general principle of striking, but it will be well to examine in detail the different strokes which are required in skating.

Different classes of stroke

1. Strokes continuing the direction of the previous curve

When taking a fresh stroke, if the trend of the new curve is in the same direction as in the case of the previous one, the second curve should be practically a continuation of the other. Thus:

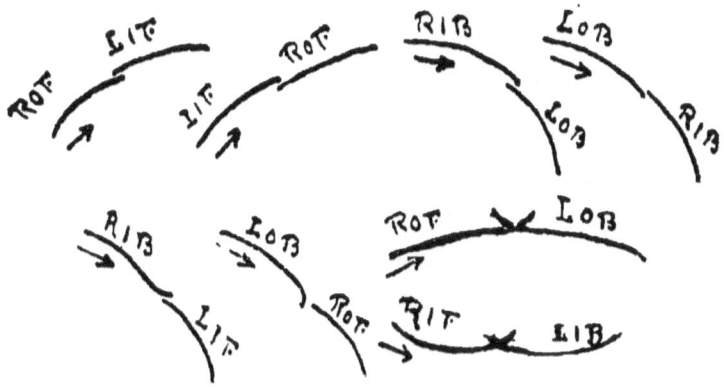

In strokes of this class from a *forward edge to a forward edge*, and from a *back edge to a back edge*, the stroke must be taken with the feet as nearly as possible parallel. Thus:

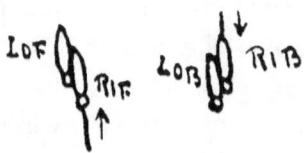

2. O F to O F, and I F to I F

In strokes from *O F to O F*, and from *I F to I F*, the foot should be put down close to the other, and slightly in advance, with the heel close to the hollow of the other foot, at an angle of rather less than 45°. Thus:

Right foot in position for fresh stroke.

3. O B to O B, and I B to I B

In strokes from *O B to O B*, and from *I B to I B*, the foot should be placed on the ice slightly behind the other, with the toe of the skate close to the hollow of the other foot, at an angle of rather less than 45°. Thus:

Right foot in position for fresh stroke.

4. Cross-rolls, O F to O F, I F to I F, O B to O B, and I B to I B

A cross-roll consists of crossing the legs to take up the fresh stroke, so that, in taking a stroke on the right leg, the foot is placed to the *outside* of the left foot, and *vice versá*. The position of the feet for the stroke is as follows:

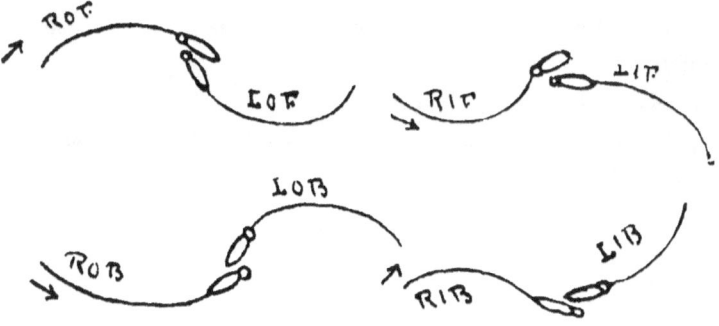

Whether skated forwards or backwards, the thrust, which is the principal motive power, is obtained from the outside instead of the inside of the blade, as in ordinary plain strokes, and the foot about to take up the fresh edge must be brought across the other either before or behind, according to the direction of progress, at a convenient angle to admit of this.

In the outside cross-roll, a *bonâ fide* outside edge is skated throughout. In the inside cross-roll, the travelling foot has to roll over on to the outside edge before placing the other foot on the ice, in order to obtain the stroke.

The crossing of the legs should be effected gradually without any jerky movement. The moment the foot leaves the ice, the leg should begin to swing forward, or back, as the case may be, at a uniform pace, regulated according to the speed of the whole movement, so as to be ready to take up the fresh stroke at the right instant. The whole movement must be quiet and smooth, and the unemployed leg when moving forwards, or backwards, must be close to the other, never being allowed to swing outwards and cross the other with a circular sweep, as is too often seen.

Skated *backwards*, both legs should be kept straight the whole time (the Mohawks and Choctaws, hereafter described, being the only other movements in skating where such is the case), and the thrust is obtained from the *toe* of the skate about to leave the ice, the leg being well braced at the moment.

The dip down when placing the foot on the ice, so often noticeable in the back cross-roll, entirely spoils the effect, and is quite unnecessary.

In skating the *inside back* cross-roll, more power can be obtained by crossing the foot over in front, instead of behind. This movement is known as the "*back scratch*."

It is skated as follows:—While travelling on the back edge, the foot which is crossed over in front must be allowed to drop on to the I B edge with a certain amount of swing in the direction of progress, while a thrust is obtained at the same time from the outside of the travelling foot as it leaves the ice, the skate rolling over to admit of the stroke being taken. Thus:

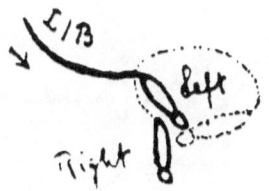

The dotted line shows the movement of the right foot before being put down.

The movement does not quite amount to a hop, as one foot actually touches the ice before the other leaves it.

The thrust is obtained from the *toe* of the skate.

Care must be taken to get very lightly on the back edge when taking up the stroke in this way.

5. *Back to forward*

In strokes from a *back edge to a forward edge*, the foot should be placed on the ice at *right angles* if an *O F edge*, and at an *obtuse angle* if an *I F edge* is to be taken up. In strokes of this class the heel, which must be close to the other foot, should be placed a little further forward than the hollow of the foot, this enabling the skater to obtain a more vigorous thrust without danger of the toe of the propelling skate slipping. Thus:

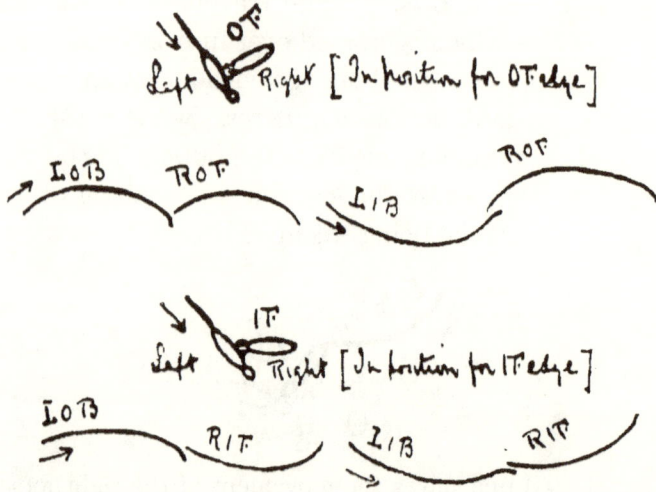

Additional power may be obtained by shifting the position of the travelling foot at the moment of striking, that, by reducing the angle, the feet may be in a more favourable position for a vigorous stroke. By adopting this plan, if an *F O stroke* is to be taken, the foot may be placed at an angle of about 45°; if an *I F stroke* is to be taken, at right angles to the other. Thus:

A. Direction of back curve.
B. Fresh position of foot when shifted.
C. Right foot in position for stroke of O F edge.

A. Direction of back curve.
B. Fresh position of foot when shifted.
C. Right foot in position for stroke of I F edge.

It must be left to the skater's own judgment when to make use of the latter method, which is not always necessary.

In all strokes from a *back to a forward edge* (except the back cross Mohawks and Choctaws,[36] which, as being acrobatic feats, need not be seriously considered), the thrust is from the inside of the skate, which has to roll over for the stroke, if not already on that edge. In the latter case, this is the moment when the position of the foot is shifted to obtain a more powerful stroke.

6. Forward to back, i.e., Mohawks and Choctaws

A stroke from a *forward edge to a back edge* is effected by means of a Mohawk or Choctaw. Such a stroke is only required in English skating when one or the other of these figures is called. There are four different strokes of this class, namely:

---

[36] Cross Mohawks and Choctaws are described on pages 79 and 99.

O F to O B, *i.e.*, Outside Mohawk.
I F to I B, *i.e.*, Inside Mohawk.

O F to I B, *i.e.*, Outside Choctaw.
I F to O B, *i.e.*, Inside Choctaw.

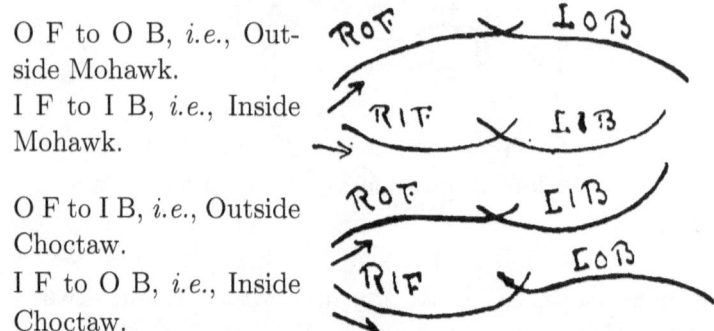

Before getting on to the back edge the shoulders must revolve by pressing back the arm on the same side as the unemployed leg, till they are approximately in the same straight line as the travelling foot, the head being allowed to follow round so that it is looking back, away from the direction of progress. For the few who can naturally spread-eagle their feet, it is then only necessary to put down the unemployed foot on the required back edge heel to heel with the other, which is then lifted from the ice.

For the large majority who lack the requisite suppleness for this simple method, the following manner of taking up the back edge is recommended, viz.:

The unemployed foot must first get hold of the ice, close to the heel of the other, with the inside of the toe of the skate, before being fairly put down. Thus:

The foot on the back edge then glides to the rear, while the other slightly changes the direction of the forward curve, as if about to make the analogous turn, resulting in the feet being approximately at right angles, toe to heel. At this moment the foot on the forward edge, instead of effecting the turn, leaves the ice, in the act of giving a thrust with a straight leg.

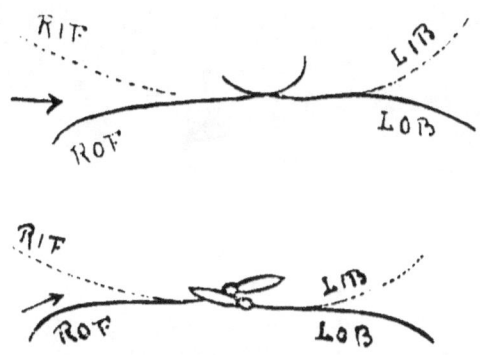

Position of feet, when foot taking up back edge gets hold of the ice with the inside of the toe of the skate.

Position of the feet at the moment of the thrust as the foot leaves the ice.

In all strokes of this class the position of the feet is practically the same, irrespective of edge, but the power of the stroke varies.

In the case of the *Outside Mohawk* and *Inside Choc-*

taw, a vigorous thrust can be obtained, which gives the skater fresh impetus, and at the same time forces him on to the outside edge.

In the case of the *Inside Mohawk*, the stroke is weaker since the skater has to remain on the inside edge. Where impetus is not required the *Inside Mohawk* may be neatly made in a different manner, consisting of placing the foot on the ice behind the other, so that the feet are nearly parallel, toe to heel. Thus:

One foot is merely lifted from the ice as the other is put down. In the case of the *Outside Choctaw*, hardly any impetus can be gained on taking up the I B edge, owing to the fact that the inclination of the body required for the fresh curve converges towards its inclination on the previous edge, as will be seen from the following diagram. Thus:

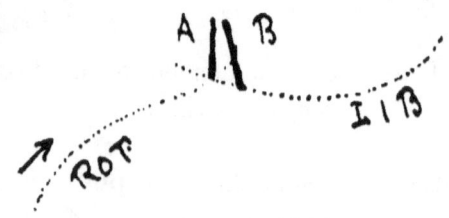

A. Inclination on O F edge.
B. Inclination on I B edge.

English Skating

This precludes the possibility of a vigorous thrust, which would force the skate taking up the back stroke on to the outside edge, resulting in a Mohawk.

Hence, sometimes, for special reasons [*e.g.*, in skating consecutive B turns[37] to a centre], some method has to be resorted to in order to gain impetus. swinging the foot over *in front*, with the toe well turned out, sot hat on dropping on to the ice the feet are toe to toe, is the usual alternative for the ordinary Choctaw. Thus:

The dotted line shows the movement of the left foot before being put down.

The instant the unemployed foot is put down on the back edge, the other leaves the ice in the act of making an O F counter, a vigorous shove from the toe of the skate as it does so giving the necessary impetus for the succeeding movement.

Mohawks and Choctaws can also be skated backwards, that is, beginning with the back edge. In this form they are merely a simple forward edge after a back edge. (See Class 5.)

---

[37]Back inside three turns; see page 95.

The O B Mohawk is merely an O B edge followed by a curve of O F.
The I B   „   „   „   „   I B edge   „   „   „   „   I F.
The O B Choctaw   „   „   „   O B edge   „   „   „   „   I F.
The I B   „   „   „   „   I B edge   „   „   „   „   O F.

Special remarks on various classes of stroke

Unemployed foot must be brought forward (except in back cross-rolls and Class 6) before being put down

In all strokes from one foot to the other, with the exception of the *back* cross-rolls (Class 4), and Mohawks and Choctaws (Class 6), it is necessary, assuming that the unemployed leg has been carried behind in the proper position, to bring forward the unemployed foot before putting it down; otherwise the skater will be unable to place his foot on the ice in the correct relative position to its fellow. The relative position of the feet when travelling on any edge being thus,

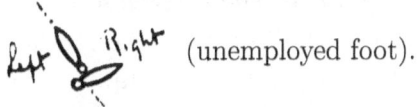 (unemployed foot).

a glance at the previous diagrams will suffice to show that such is the case. This bringing forward of the foot is best effected by bringing forward the hip of the unemployed leg, allowing the foot to follow. It is more especially necessary to pay attention to this when taking up a forward stroke after a back edge, since it is contrary to the instinct of the beginner to bring the foot forward in this case, his inclination being rather to reach out backwards with it, with the result that the fresh stroke is taken up too far from the other foot. After a forward edge the unemployed foot is brought forward instinctively.

Special remarks on Classes 2 and 3

Differences in principle between outside and inside edge skated on alternate feet

As regards strokes comprised in Classes 2 and 3, that is, *forward edge to forward edge*, and *back edge to back edge*, it should be noted that there is a marked difference in principle between skating a plain outside edge on alternate feet, and an inside edge.

In both cases, the thrust from the propelling foot is from the inside edge, the result being that whether an outside or an inside edge is to be taken up by the other foot, that is, whatever the direction of the fresh curve, the inclination of the body for the stroke is the same. When an outside edge is taken up, at the moment of the stroke the inclination is towards the centre of the circle of which the fresh curve is a portion of the circumference, the propelling leg being to the outside. In the case of the inside edge, at the moment of the stroke the body is leaning away from the centre of the circle of which the fresh curve is a portion of the circumference, the propelling leg being within the circumference of the circle. Or, in other words, in skating the outside edge, the body is able to swing over from right to left, or *vice versâ*, just before the stroke, the inclination of the body after thus rolling over, in order to obtain the thrust from the inside of the skate, being that required for the new curve; whereas, in skating the inside edge, the necessity of remaining on that edge for the stroke prevents the body from swinging over, and so assuming, beforehand, the inclination required for the fresh edge. The inclination of the body is therefore correct for the outside, and incorrect for the inside, edge.

The following diagrams will enable the reader to see at a glance that such is the case.

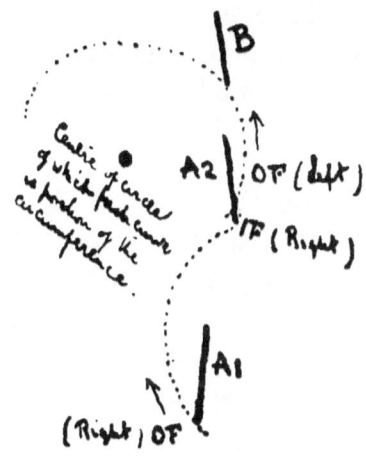

A1. Inclination of body on O F edge on right foot.
A2. Inclination of body after rolling over on to the I F edge for the stroke.
B. Inclination of body on O F edge on left foot.

It follows from the correct inclination of the body for the outside edge previous to the stroke that it is easy to get hard and firm on the edge from the very beginning.

English Skating

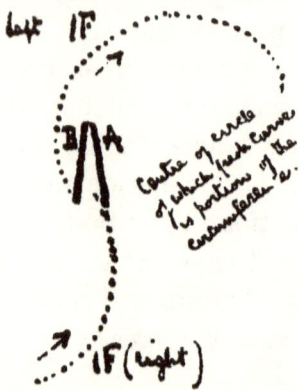

A. Inclination of body on I F edge on right foot. (The dotted line shows the previous track.)

B. Inclination the body will have to assume on taking up a stroke of I F edge on the left foot.

Now if the skater on taking up the fresh stroke of I F gets fairly on the edge "*ab initio*,"[38] his inclination must be "*ab initio*" as indicated by B. At the same time, the thrust being from the inside of the blade of the right skate, the previous inclination indicated by A is that required for the stroke. Hence at the moment of striking the body must be simultaneously inclined in the two different directions indicated by A and B, which is absurd. This dilemma results in the compromise of a vertical position with both ankles twisted so as to be on the inside of both skates, unless the skater beggars the question by keeping the feet well separated at the stroke, which is what is usually done, though contrary to all principles of correct striking. Hence the accepted

---

[38]"From the beginning."

postulate that the skate must at once bite the ice on a true edge, irrespective of all other considerations, if strictly adhered to, here leads to difficulties.

How to skate an inside edge on alternate feet, so as to avoid a forced position of the feet

In taking up an inside edge, therefore, whether forwards or backwards, on alternate feet, the following method is suggested as preferable, namely, that in the first instance the skater should place his foot on the ice on the flat of the blade, the feet being close together in the prescribed position, and continue on the flat of his skate until the body is free to adopt the proper inclination for the inside curve, that is, until one foot is clear of the other, when he should get fairly on the edge. By this simple expedient, by the time the feet are clear of one another, which is the point where the foot is usually placed on the ice in the first instance, the skater has already utilised the initial part of the thrust which is wasted when the feet are apart, while avoiding the strained position objected to when the principle of approximation of the feet is observed.

The difference in effect between the use of the initial part of the thrust, and its omission, is much the same as that between getting hold of the water, when rowing, with the blade of the oar well behind the rowlock, so as to row the stroke fairly through, and cutting the first part of the stroke, thereby merely obtaining a jerky snatch at the water when half the stroke should be already rowed out.

Many skaters endeavour to compensate for the loss

of the initial part of the thrust by lunging on to the new edge with something very like a stamp of the foot, a habit which cannot be too strongly condemned.

Where the principle of approximation of the feet is observed, it is the superstition that it is a crime not to force the skate to bite the ice on a hard edge the moment the foot is put down, irrespective of other considerations, alone, which needlessly converts a perfectly simple into a somewhat difficult movement.

Superstitions, however, die hard, since they grow round time-honoured maxims which by long usage have become accepted postulates of the art, to question which is regarded by the conscientiously orthodox as sheer heresy.

The above considerations are, however, worthy of the attention of those who permit themselves greater latitude. There appears to be no logical reason why the inside edge thus skated should be regarded as a faulty movement, owing to the fact that the whole of each curve is not *bonâ fide* inside edge, so long as no such objection is raised in the case of the outside edge, where the skate necessarily rolls over on to the inside edge at the end of each curve to enable the stroke to be taken. If a *bonâ fide* edge, throughout, is to be the only criterion of sound skating, then the ordinary outside edge on alternate feet should be discarded, and the movement only be skated with the cross-roll. This would be an even greater mistake than gratuitously creating difficulties in the case of the inside edge; but if the latter be a *sine quâ non*, logic demands that the former be equally imperative. The fact that it is possible to skate a *bonâ fide* inside edge, throughout, by a forced effort, does not, however, prove the desirability of doing so, since anything int he nature of an acrobatic feat is objectionable in the English style, and the small piece of fault edge may therefore be allowed to pass unchallenged. It would be pedantic to characterise it as a serpentine, since the skate is fairly on the inside edge before the propelling foot actually leaves the ice.

In the case of the inside edge the faulty edge is at the commencement; in the case of the outside edge, at the completion of the curve, and no valid reason can be adduced for stigmatising the one as wrong, while approving the other. The same applies in skating an inside edge after an outside edge, since the skate has to roll over on to the inside edge to obtain the stroke.

The following diagrams illustrate the difference between the marks on the ice of an outside edge and an inside edge, skated as recommended.

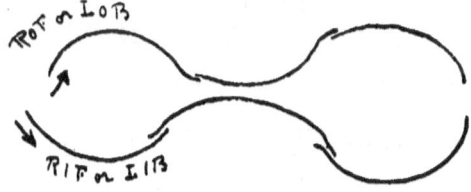

Special remarks on Class 4

The outside edge skated with the cross-roll has one feature in common with the ordinary plain inside edge on alternate feet, namely, that the propelling leg is inclined away from the centre of the circle of which the fresh curve is a portion of the circumference, being within the latter, but, unlike the ordinary inside edge, owing to the crossing of the legs, it admits of a true edge being taken up at once without forcing the ankle into a strained position.

Suppose, however, for the sake of argument, that taking up the outside edge thus necessitated a strained position which could be relieved by the simple expedient of not getting fairly on to the edge at once, then common sense would suggest the adoption of the latter method, though the severely orthodox would doubtless protest. It would, however, be illogical to condemn the movement as faulty, while admitting the inside cross-roll to be *bonâ fide*, in spite of the fact that the foot has to roll over on to the outside edge before the other is put down, in order to obtain the stroke; just as it would be illogical to take exception to the plain inside edge skated as previously suggested, unless the plain inside edge were likewise condemned.

Utility of inside cross-roll

The cross-roll is usually assumed to mean the *outside* edge skated as described, indeed the majority of skaters ignore the existence of any other.

The inside edge cross-roll, though lacking the essential characteristic of the former, namely, a true edge throughout, and seldom skated, should not, however, be neglected in practice, since this stroke may be utilised in combined figure-skating, in order to dispense with the ordinary, and somewhat ungainly, alternate stroke of inside edge. The thrust being from the outside of the blade in skating the cross-roll, this stroke can be conveniently used likewise after a curve of *outside* edge, whether forwards or backwards, the second curve being practically a continuation of the first.

Objection to the ordinary stroke of I B

It is more especially in the case of the I B edge that is desirable to have some alternative, so as to avoid when possible the ordinary stroke, since the combination of the turned-in toes, and the strained position while forcing the foot on to the inside edge in spite of the wrong inclination of the body, when skated in the orthodox manner, produce an effect too suggestive of a clown at a circus for grace. If the recommendation to put down the foot on the flat of the blade before getting fairly on to the inside edge be followed, the movement, it is true, is less objectionable, but still leaves something to be desired from an æsthetic point of view.

Alternative methods of skating I B edge

Taking up the inside back edge as in the I B cross-roll is, as already shown, one alternative. A second alternative consists of crossing the leg over in front (*i.e.*, the step known as the "*back scratch*," already described).[39] This stroke likewise can be conveniently employed whatever the previous edge.

---

[39] See page 56.

English Skating

When the "back scratch" should be used

After a stroke of O B edge, the "back scratch" causes the skater to travel on a curve to the inside of the previous one, as will be seen from the diagram on the following page.

This is the best method to employ when a B turn[40] has to be made at the centre after "twice-back,"[41] if, as recommended by some authorities, the intention is to go as direct as possible to the centre, instead of continuing to circle on the circumference.

The ordinary stroke of I B after O B, to obtain which the travelling foot has to roll over to the inside edge for the thrust, has the opposite effect, as will be seen from the position of the feet. Thus:

---

[40] A back inside three turn; see page 95.

[41] Twice back is a figure in English style skating that is similar to a pair of modern waltz threes. The skater does a forward outside three turn followed by a back outside edge on the other foot, then steps forward and repeats it. See page 160.

When the I B cross-roll should be used

Taking up the I B edge after a stroke of O B, in the same manner as in skating the I B cross-roll, is the best method to employ when skating "inside twice-back,"[42] since in this movement the skater must keep on the circumference, neither turning in towards the centre, nor receding too far from it, and, in taking up the stroke in this way, while avoiding the former, which is the tendency of the "back scratch," he steers clear of the other extreme, which is the objection to the ordinary stroke. In skating this movement, the feet should be very slightly crossed, being almost toe to heel. Thus:

The thrust is obtained, as in the case of the O B cross-roll, from the toe.

The ordinary stroke of inside back edge, however, is easier than the alternative methods, which require a considerable amount of practice in order to obtain the same power. When the ordinary stroke is used, care should be taken to make it as little uncouth as may be, by putting down the foot very close to the other with the heel only slightly turned out. A comparison of the

---

[42] Twice back with inside threes instead of outside threes. See page 160.

foregoing diagrams will suffice to show the difference in the direction of the new curve, according to the manner of taking up the stroke.

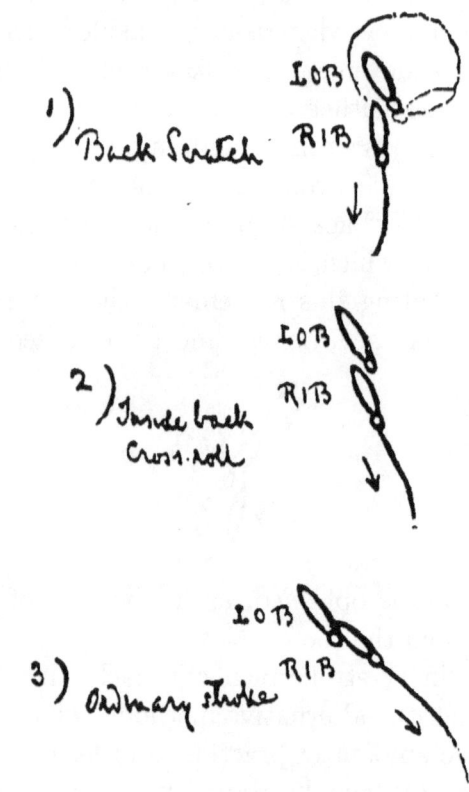

Special remarks on Class 5

How to prepare for I F edge after I B edge

As regards strokes comprised under Class 5, namely, *back edge to forward edge*, the *I F edge after an I B edge* is the stroke that is most often taken up incorrectly, the skater usually placing the feet heel to heel at some little distance apart, in which attitude it is impossible to get a really powerful stroke, the foot on the I B edge being apt to slip as the shove is given.

The beginner must therefore be careful to strike in the proper way as previously described. Before taking up the fresh stroke, the body must slue round in preparation for the forward edge, in precisely the same was as if the analogous turn (I B bracket) were contemplated, and the moment to take up the fresh stroke is the moment the turn could have been effected. Until the beginner is familiar with the turns, he must content himself with remembering to force back the shoulder corresponding to the unemployed leg.

How to prepare for O F edge after O B edge

Similarly, in taking up an *O F edge after an O B edge*, the stroke should not be taken till the body has gone through the preparation for a D turn,[43] and could at that moment effect it. In this case, too, forcing back the shoulder corresponding to the unemployed leg will answer the purpose, for those who are not familiar with the turns.

Strokes from back edge to forward edge, the trend of both curves being the same

The position of the feet for strokes from a *back edge to a forward edge*, as given previously (Class 5), would

---

[43] A back outside three turn; see page 95.

appear at first sight to preclude the possibility of the fresh curve continuing the direction of the previous one, where the trend of both is the same. This is *not*, however, the case, since in taking up a forward after a back edge, whether the stroke be of this class or not, the preparation of the body for the fresh edge just previous to the stroke causes a slight deviation of direction corresponding to the increased curvature, or change of direction, before the cusp, in making the analogous turn, the body having in both cases to make similar preparation. This deviation in the case of strokes of the class under discussion, viz., where the trend of the new curve is a continuation of the previous one, requires that the next edge should be taken up at an angle to the actual direction at the moment of the stroke, in order that the foot may continue the direction of the original curve.

The following diagrams illustrate the cusp in the turns in question, and the corresponding deviation in strokes requiring similar preparation.

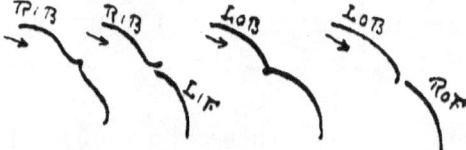

In all strokes from a *back to a forward edge*, as well as from a *forward to a back edge* (Mohawks and Choctaws), this deviation from the original direction of the curve exists, and is due to the same cause, namely, the preparation of the body as if about to skate the analogous turn, the other foot only taking up the fresh edge at the instant when the turn would otherwise be effected.

This particular feature of striking will be better appreciated after studying the "Principle of Skating Turns," where the analogy between turns and their corresponding two-footed movements is pointed out. In strokes from a *forward edge to a forward edge*, and from a *back edge to a back edge*, an apparent deviation from the direction of the original curve may likewise be seen on examining the marks on the ice; but this is merely due to the action of the foot while giving the thrust, and has no connection with preparation as if to make an analogous turn.

Special remarks on Class 6

Cross-Mohawks and Cross-Choctaws

Mohawks and Choctaws can be skated with the contrary motion, and are called *Cross-Mohawks* and *Cross-Choctaws*, but they are rather acrobatic feats than recognised essential movements, especially when commenced on a back edge. Those, however, who have a fancy for occasionally indulging in grotesque movements of little utility may like to understand their nature.

The subsequent edge can easily be taken up, with the proper rotation, after the first part of the movement, by allowing the foot to make a turn before the other is put down. Thus:

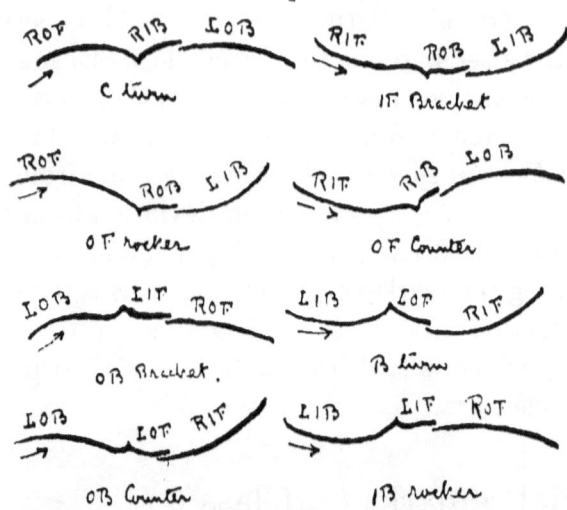

To convert these movements into Cross-Mohawks and Cross-Choctaws, and back Cross-Mohawks and back Cross-Choctaws, it is necessary in every case to suppress the turn, the change of foot following at once after the first curve, which is impossible without a jump or a contortion. Such movements come under the head of antics, which need not claim serious attention.

Eights to a centre

Two forwards entire

Having studied the various ways of striking according to circumstances, the beginner is in a position to practise eights to a centre on all edges, and it will be well here to point out a few facts for his information and guidance.

Nature of so-called eights. Manner of Skating

A so-called eight to a centre, in skating which the ordinary stroke, and not the cross-roll, is usually employed, is not a perfect representation of the figure after which it is called, neither half being a perfect circle, owing to the necessity of avoiding the centre.

Each half of the eight is technically termed "*forward entire*," and since the figure is chiefly useful as a preliminary practice for combined figure-skating, the beginner must here be so far initiated as to enable him to practise it correctly. The skater, then, should commence on the right foot, so that the centre is to the inside of the curve to be skated, but on returning to the centre he should keep it to the outside of the curve he is on; or, in technical terms, he should commence on the "off-side," and return on the "near-side" of the centre. This enables him to commence a half-eight, or forward entire, in like manner on the left foot; what is the "near-side" for one foot being the "off-side for the other on the same edge.

Cause of scraping when on an edge

When first commencing eights to a centre, and even in free skating, beginners are sometimes conscious of a scrape, as if something were impeding the blade from travelling freely. The usual suggestion, when advice is asked, is that the beginner should change his blades, as they are probably buckled.

A blade which is not true, however slightly out of the straight, will, it is true, often produce this effect. In nine cases out of ten, however, the fault lies with the skater. This cause of the scrape is that the beginner has not thoroughly realised that the skate must eventually complete a circle if on a true edge, being incapable of travelling otherwise than in curves, unless on the flat of the blade. In his anxiety to come round and reach the centre, he keeps trying to point his toe in the desired direction, instead of letting the curve he is on ultimately take him there. He is, in fact, perpetually trying to turn the skate broadside to the true direction of the curve, which results in a scrape, and impedes it from travelling freely.

In some cases this fault arises from want of confidence, which prevents the beginner from getting fairly on to the edge, and he endeavours to travel on a curve by this action of the foot, while practically on the flat of the skate.

The inclination of the body alone must regulate the curve, the foot being quiescent, its function being merely to support the skater.

Special feature of inside eights

In skating inside eights *forwards*, the skater, it may be pointed out, should take the fresh stroke just *before* arriving at the centre. Since the foot about to leave the ice is to the inside of the circle to be skated, that is, between the other foot and the centre, which it is therefore apt to displace in the act of giving the thrust, unless lifted from the ice before reaching it. In skating inside eights *backwards*, on the other hand, the stroke should not be taken till the centre is passed, to avoid the risk of disturbing it, either during the stroke, or as the foot is brought to the rear immediately after.

In skating outside eights, whether forwards or backwards, the stroke can be taken at the centre itself, the propelling leg being to the outside.

Head not brought round into correct position for edge till half the circle is completed; especially on back edges

It should further be noted that in skating eights the head should not be fairly brought round into the correct position for the edge till half the circle is completed. This is more especially necessary when the movement is backwards. Indeed the principle of not bringing the head fairly round till half the curve to be skated is completed should be observed in skating all edges, especially backwards, whether a complete circle is to be made or not; otherwise the skater will be thrown too hard on the edge to ensure perfect control over the movement.

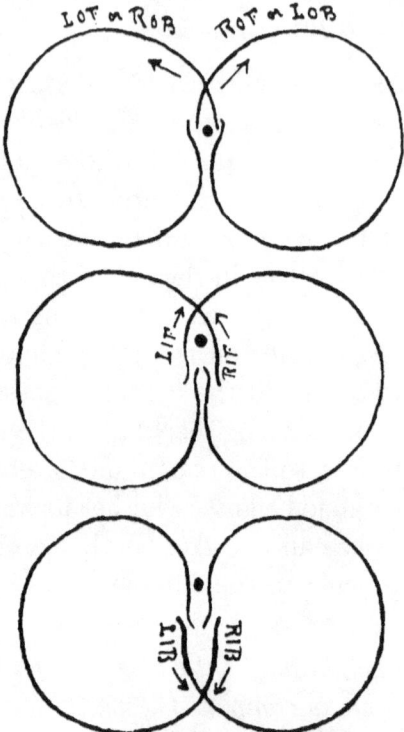

Diagrams of eights to a centre skated with ordinary stroke, *i.e.*, without crossing the legs.

The head, too, must never be brought round suddenly, since any abrupt movement is liable to disturb the balance.

Eights skated with the cross-roll

Eights may also be skated with the cross-roll, but they are necessarily smaller. In the case of inside eights so skated, there is no objection to skating right up to the centre, since there is no danger of disturbing it on taking up the fresh stroke, the thrust being with the outside of the blade, away from, and not towards, the centre.

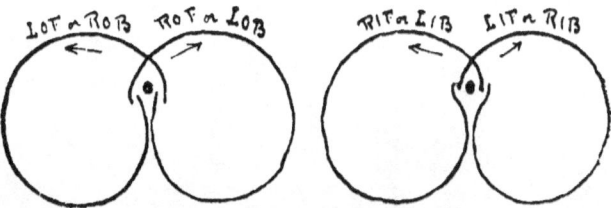

Diagrams of eights skated with the cross-roll.

Concluding remarks

It being understood that the shoulders and arms have to adapt themselves *beforehand* to the requirements of the succeeding curve, it is needless to lay down elaborate rules as to the change of position in every case, since a moment's reflection will enable the beginner, knowing as he does already the correct attitude for the curve about to be skated, to make the necessary alteration, and a little experience will enable him to prepare instinctively for the new edge.

The correct manner of taking up a fresh stroke, however, does not appear to be a matter of instinct to the same extent, and it is therefore necessary to impress on skaters the great importance of the approximation of the feet, in the correct relative position, before placing the foot on the ice. Failing this, no even moderately powerful stroke can be obtained without exaggerated lunging, which is merely misapplied energy, and produces an appearance of effort, without any adequate result.

Having learnt the edges, and how to strike correctly, the beginner, no longer an absolute tyro, is ready to study the "Principle of Skating Turns," in which a system to some extent differing from the time-honoured method of making turns is brought to his notice, whereby one principle is applicable to all, and the task of learning them consequently facilitated. This will complete the preparation necessary before approaching the subject of combined figure-skating.

Though the turns should not be learnt till the four edges can be creditably skated, it is a mistake to postpone them till such absolute proficiency has been acquired that great power and a masterly style are conspicuous. General improvement can be made while learning the turns, otherwise the disproportion between a skater's capacity for simple edges and incapacity for turns becomes too marked, and it is disappointing to find that a man, whose general style gives hopes of better things, is quite incapable of taking part in a simple combined figure of the most elementary description. Skating does not consist of edges alone, and however fine and large they may be they are only the first step to higher things. Moreover, when beginners are restricted exclusively to edges for too long a time, and the turns are relegated to a dim future, they are apt to get an exaggerated idea of their difficulty, and approach them with an amount of apprehension which no movement in English skating really calls for.

The principle of thoroughness which insists that one thing shall be completely mastered before another is attempted can be carried too far, in skating at all events, since the attempt to learn a comparatively difficult movement often gives increased facility in an easier one, which was previously skated with an effort. The essential point with a view to combined figure-skating, which is the *raison d'être* of the English style, is equality throughout. It is of no use being able to skate edges alone, in however masterly a way, and but of little use being able to skate one or two turns with perfect facility, if the rest are neglected. All are required, for there is nothing more vexatious than being restricted to a limited *répertoire* in a combined figure, because there are certain movements that one, or more, of the performers cannot skate.

Instead of shirking certain turns on account of their difficulty, extra practice should be devoted to them, as all must be skated with facility. Inequality in the turns means inequality in pace, easy turns being approached boldly, and executed without loss of speed, the more difficult ones slowly and without confidence, with a further diminution of speed resulting from the turn itself. This variation in the speed of travelling produces a want of go, and an absence of the evenness and uniformity of pace, which is one of the beauties of combined figure-skating. The study of the "Principle of Skating Turns" is therefore recommended to the beginner as soon as the four edges can be skated in a fairly creditable manner.

The cover of Henry C. Lowther's *Principle of Skating Turns* (London: Horace Cox, 1900).

Preface

The object of the following treatise on the principle of skating turns is to put forward the theory therein developed, called the "hip *versus* shoulder" system.

It is not intended for the absolute tyro, since it assumes that the reader is already conversant with the technicalities of skating; but, since it treats the subject with which it deals in a new light, it is hoped that its perusal may be of some interest to skaters in general, whether they approve or condemn the theory therein set forth.

Though the theory, as such, is new, the principle is not unfrequently put into practice by experts, though apparently unconsciously, since their advice to beginners invariably consists of the time-honoured precepts.

It is needless here to touch on the advantages claimed for the "hip *versus* shoulder" system, since they are sufficiently explained in the treatise itself.

It is hoped that the skating public may prove rather to be imbued with the desire of the Athenians of old to "hear some new thing" than impregnated with the spirit of the doctrine "omne ignotum pro horribile."[44]

It is with this prayer that the following treatise is submitted to their criticism.

HENRY C. LOWTHER

Berne, August 15, 1900.

---

[44]"Everything unknown is to be feared."

Movements required in English figure skating

Before studying the following treatise on the principle of skating turns, the skater should make himself familiar with the names and nature of the different movements required in English figure skating.

Turns

Names of turns and nature of

There are sixteen turns to be skated on either foot. They are the following:

[N. B.—O F is an abbreviation of "Outside forward." I F "Inside forward." O B "Outside back." I B "Inside back."]

SIMPLE TURNS.	BRACKET TURNS.

A turn I F to O B
B " I B to O F
C " O F to I B
D " O B to I F

These turns are called "threes."

The four corresponding bracket turns are skated on the same edges, but the rotation is in the contrary direction. They may therefore be regarded as Counter Threes.

Rockers.	Counters.

I F to I B
I B to I F
O F to O B
O B to O F

The name given to these turns is an abbreviation of the original name "Counter rocking turn." Counters are skated on the same edges as the corresponding rockers, but the rotation is in the contrary direction.

Turns classified according to the direction of rotation

The above may be classified under the following groups, as a guide to the direction of the rotation, and consequently the preparation required for the turn.[45]

Q's and reverse Q's

Q's consist of any turn preceded by a change of edge.

Reverse Q's consist of any turn followed by a change of edge.

Unless a simple turn, the word *rocker, counter,* or *bracket* must precede the Q to explain the nature of the movement.

---

[45]See the table on page 97.

English Skating

Forward turns
$\left\{\begin{array}{l}\text{A turn}\\\text{I F rocker}\\\text{O F rocker}\\\text{O F bracket}\end{array}\right.$
The shoulders rotate by pressing back the arm corresponding to the unemployed leg.
$\left\{\begin{array}{l}\text{D turn}\\\text{O B rocker}\\\text{I B counter}\\\text{I B bracket}\end{array}\right.$

$\left\{\begin{array}{l}\text{C turn}\\\text{O F rocker}\\\text{I F counter}\\\text{I F bracket}\end{array}\right.$
The shoulders rotate by pressing back the arm corresponding to the employed leg.
$\left\{\begin{array}{l}\text{B turn}\\\text{I B rocker}\\\text{O B counter}\\\text{O B bracket}\end{array}\right.$

Back turns

Unless the word *inside* is used, it is understood that the movement, whether forwards or backwards, is commenced on the outside edge; and unless the word *back* is used, that the movement is begun on a forward edge.

Multiple turns

Two or more turns may be joined together and skated in sequence by the same foot. These are called "multiple turns."

Mohawks and Choctaws

A *Mohawk* consists of changing from a forward edge on one foot to the corresponding back edge on the other, practically continuing the same curve.

INSIDE MOHAWK

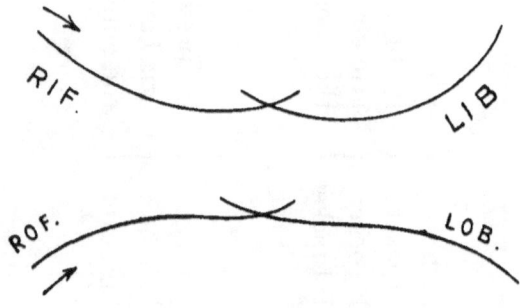

OUTSIDE MOHAWK

The movement may be regarded as a one-footed Spread-Eagle, the foot on the forward edge completing its task before the other beings, instead of the two feet travelling at the same time heel to heel.

The Inside Mohawk skated backwards is merely an ordinary I B and I F.

The Outside Mohawk skated backwards is merely an ordinary O B and O F.

A *Choctaw* differs from a Mohawk in that the other edge is taken up by the unemployed foot.

INSIDE CHOCTAW   OUTSIDE CHOCTAW

The Inside Choctaw skated backwards is merely an ordinary O B and I F.

The Outside Choctaw skated backwards is merely an ordinary I B and O F.

The *Cross Mohawks* and *Cross Choctaws* are rather acrobatic curiosities than movements required for English figure skating. Those commenced on the O F edge necessitate rotation as though an ordinary simple turn were to be made; those commenced on the I F edge, as though a Counter or Bracket were to be skated, the converse being the case when the back edge is skated first.

Principle of skating turns

The preparation for all turns is the same in principle. The skater should be easy and natural, in the correct position for the curve on which he is travelling before beginning to prepare for the turn.

It is assumed that the skater is familiar with the essential features of good form, in the English style, when travelling on any edge, viz. :—

> Sideways attitude of the body.
> Face turned in the direction of progress.
> Uprightness of carriage.
> Straightness of the employed leg.
> Approximation of the feet.

By the "correct position for the curve on which the skater is travelling" is meant the fulfilment of these requirements.

Two methods of skating turns

There are two distinct methods of effecting a turn.

1. Old system of revolving hips and shoulders together

The usual receipt, which has the authority of many excellent skaters, both past and present, consists of revolving simultaneously head, shoulders, and hips, the foot alone making the turn subsequently, the "screw-round-everything-you've-got-for-all-you're worth" system, as it is sometimes facetiously called.

2. *"Hip v. shoulder" system*

The present treatise is intended to bring to the notice of skaters in general another method, which in one respect is radically different, in that the hips are not allowed to follow the rotation of the shoulders, until the foot whips round.

The merit claimed for this method is that greater speed is acquired by the turn, a matter of such importance that, if once generally recognized, a system productive of such a result would need no further justification.

Careful and critical observation of the performance of first-class skaters tends to show that the method here advocated is in not a few cases put in practice, though apparently unconsciously, since no theory respecting turns, in any way subversive of the time-honoured receipt, has hitherto been formulated.

As far as the actual making of the turn is concerned, neither method can be pronounced the better, clean, smart turns resulting equally from both, when illustrated by an expert. It is by considering the subsequent effect of the turn, alone, that it is possible to decide in favour of one or the other, and as additional impetus is, it is here maintained, acquired by the "*hip* v. *shoulder*" system, as it may be called, it is the latter which is recommended to those who have not already formed their style of skating.

The "hip v. shoulder" method, therefore, is fully dealt with in this treatise, that skaters may realise the difference between the two systems, and it is hoped prove for themselves that additional speed is gained by putting into practice the principles here explained. The effect of making the turn thus is particularly noticeable after a forward rocker, and an A turn. The difficulty of holding the edge after the former is greatly reduced, and the tendency to curl in on the back edge, after the latter, entirely disappears.

Essential features of preparation for turn

Every turn, then, should be effected by the *hip-play*, which is by far the most important factor, working against the *revolution of the shoulders*, the former resisting the latter till the moment comes for the foot to whip round.

Method of rotating shoulders

The shoulders should revolve by pressing back the proper arm, right arm if to the right, left arm if to the left. This arm may be termed the "*rotating arm*," and while used to rotate the shoulders should be kept extended, though not stretched out away from the body, with the elbow turned in, that is, thumb outwards.

The reason for adopting this method of making the upper part of the body revolve is to avoid the tendency to round the back and hollow the chest, which is the objection to the usual receipt of bringing forward the other shoulder. Moreover, the rotation of the shoulders is thus produced much more quietly, without the visible effort which is usually too conspicuous where the latter principle is adhered to, since this often results in a very marked sweep of the arms, first in one direction, during the preparation for the turn, then in the other, as the turn is effected, as though the skater were vigorously wielding an imaginary scythe. This mowing round of the body with the arms produces an appearance of effort and difficulty which detracts from the merit of the performance, however faultless in other respects the turn may be.

This defect is at once remedied by the method here suggested of quietly, but firmly, pressing back the rotating arm. The shoulders revolve just as effectually, and the counter movement of the arms at the turn is much less marked.

Phases of preparation for any turn

1. Proper hip brought forward and position of head where necessary altered

The preparation for every turn is commenced by bringing well *forward* the *hip* on the same side as the rotating arm. [N.B.—If not the hip of the employed leg, this is effected by forcing back the latter, since in all cases the *hip of the leg on which the skater is travelling is the master hip.*]

The *head* should be looking in the direction of the turn, but it may be allowed to follow the rotation of the shoulders just sufficiently to avoid stiffness, if it is already in position. Where the head has to be brought right round before the turn is effected, as in the case of the B turn, I B rocker, O B counter, and O B bracket, it should be brought round half way simultaneously with the bringing forward of the hip, before the shoulders begin to rotate, but then be kept stationary till the rotation has commenced, eventually following round with the shoulders.

2. Shoulders revolve, the hips meanwhile resisting rotation

The proper hip having been brought forward and the head brought round half way, if not originally looking in the direction of the turn, the *shoulders* then revolve by pressing back the rotating arm, the hips meanwhile resisting this rotation as long as possible, on no account being allowed to follow round with the shoulders, which should be made to revolve to the full extent of which they are capable without shifting the foot, that is, until they are approximately in the same straight line as the travelling foot.

To resist this rotation an effort should be made to bring forward, still more, the hip of the leg corresponding to the rotating arm as the shoulder on the same side is forced back, care being taken not to allow the play of the hips to shift the unemployed leg from its proper place. Or, in other words, the shoulders revolve in one direction and the hips make a strong effort to revolve in the other.

3. Tension relieved by snapping back hip and reversing arms, resulting in whipping round of the foot

When the hips can no longer resist the rotation of the upper part of the body the tension is relieved by *smartly* bringing back the hip that was forced forward (if not the hip of the employed leg, this is effected by smartly bringing forward the latter, which is, as stated, the master hip) and by *smartly* reversing the position of the arms at the same time; that is, the rotating arm comes across the body and the other goes back. The latter movement should, however, as far as possible, be disguised, the arms not being allowed to come back with a vigorous sweep in the manner previously alluded to as suggestive of mowing, since the effectiveness of the movement is dependent on its smartness rather than its extent. The result will be the whipping round of the foot at the same moment, and the turn is effected.

In the case of turns, where the rotating arm and the master hip are the same side, the attitude is correct for the resulting edge when the foot whips round; but when the rotating arm is the opposite side to the master hip the shoulders and arms are in the wrong position after the turn, necessitating further rotation of the shoulders, and a second reversal of the arms, the latter this time being a smooth and deliberate process. If the resulting edge is a back edge the head also has to be brought round. (For illustrative diagrams, see pages 116 and 117.)

General remarks

Whole process of preparation and execution of turn takes about three seconds

Though it is necessary to give in detail each phase of the process, involving somewhat lengthy explanations, the reader must not get the mistaken idea that the preparation for a turn is a long and laborious operation, since about three seconds suffice, from the initial phase till the whipping round of the foot, unless travelling at high speed, when a longer time should be allowed. Neither is there any interval between one phase and another, which would give a jerky appearance, the different phases, rather, merging imperceptibly one into the other, and the whole revolving itself into one perfectly smooth movement, without any suspicion of spasmodic effort.

Hip play always effected by master hip, i.e., hip of employed leg

The hip play, which, as already stated, is by far the most important factor in making turns, is in all cases effected by shifting the hip of the leg on which the skater is travelling, this being the master hip. When, therefore, the rotating arm is on the same side as the employed leg, as in the C turn, it is the hip of the latter that is forced forward; when the rotating arm is on the opposite side to the employed leg, as in the A turn, the hip of the latter is forced back, whereby the hip of the unemployed leg necessarily comes forward, the forcing back of one hip being practically the same thing as bringing forward the other. By consciously bringing forward the hip of the unemployed leg, however, the hip play is more conspicuous, and the displacement of the unemployed foot a probable contingency. It is for this reason that the hip of the leg on which the skater is travelling should always be regarded as the master hip.

Similarly, when the hip which was brought forward is smartly brought back to effect the turn, if not the hip of the leg on which the skater is travelling, it is the latter which produces this result by coming smartly forward.

The skater should endeavour to make all turns without any appearance of effort, or elaborate preparation, and, once more let it be repeated, that it is only by attaching due importance to hip play that, while doing justice to the different phases of preparation, he can so tone down every movement, other than that of the hips, as to disguise the preparation previous to the turn, and the help derived from the shifting of the arms.

Principle, and object of making the hip work against the shoulder

The principle here explained of making the hip work against the shoulder is the principle of "reculer pour mieux sauter"[46]; the hips have eventually to be brought smartly back in the opposite direction, and straining away from their ultimate goal gives a certain power of rebound, without which the turn is sure to be slug-

---

[46]"Back off to better jump," i.e., make a strategic withdrawal.

gish; just as in delivering a blow the arm is first drawn back before shooting it out, in order to render the blow more effective. The result of the smart bringing round of the hips and foot simultaneously is that a certain additional weight is suddenly thrown on to the new curve, for which the shoulders are already in position, thus increasing the momentum, and enabling the skater to gain fresh impetus by the turn; whereas, if the foot alone has to follow, after the weight of shoulders and hips has been slowly brought into position for the new edge, this is not the case to the same extent. It will be seen that there is an analogy between the use of the hips in making a turn and the use of the weight of the body in taking a fresh stroke. In both cases there is a momentary drawing back in order to come forward, in the one case the movement being horizontal, in the other vertical, and the object is in both cases the same, namely, to obtain additional momentum. The action of delivering a horizontal, as compared with an overhand service at tennis, fairly illustrates the difference between the two movements.

Preparation should be deliberate, but turn itself very smart

In all turns, the preparation should be made deliberately, about three seconds, as already stated, sufficing for this, unless travelling at high speed, but the turn itself cannot be effected too smartly, since a sluggish turn will suffice to neutralise the advantage to be gained by making turns in the manner here recommended, and, at the moment of turning, the body should be *drawn up to its full height.* This is the moment when the body comes up to the vertical, as at the instant of changing the direction from forwards to backwards, or *vice-versâ,* the skater pivots round on the flat of the blade.

All turns executed on flat of blade

No turn can be made, exclusive of "kickers," which are not, properly speaking, turns, without getting momentarily on the flat of the skate. This is evident in the case of all turns involving a change of edge, as it is clearly necessary to pass over the flat of the blade to get from one edge to the other, and at that instant the body is necessarily vertical. This is the moment when the change of direction is effected.

In the case of rockers and counters, where there is no change of edge (the apparent serpentine after and before these turns respectively not really constituting a change of edge, but being in separable from the movement which the skate has to execute, as is now generally understood), the question might be raised whether this necessity exists.

Whatever theorists may have to say on this head, it is practically impossible to change the direction from forwards to backwards, or *vice-versâ,* without serious loss of speed, without allowing the body to come up to the vertical, that is, without being momentarily on the flat of the skate.

Forward turns approached on heel

All *forward turns* should be *approached* very upright, and hence, *well on the heel*. The slight retardation of the foot occasioned by the accentuation of the curve before the cusp has a tendency to throw the body forward, which affects the movement to the extent of just easing the weight off the heel as the foot whips round, with the result that the turn is made on the centre of the blade.

Back turns approached on centre of blade

All *back turns* should be approached *on the centre of the blade*. Here, again, the effect of the slight retardation of the foot, occasioned by the accentuation of the curve before the cusp is felt, with the result that the weight is thrown slightly back as the foot whips round.

From the foregoing it will be seen that turns should not be intentionally made on the toe or heel, but, travelling in the prescribed attitude, the turn is made on the part of the skate dictated by the movement and the upright carriage of the body.

It will be found that, provided the body is perfectly upright on approaching forward turns, and does not lean forward on approaching back turns, as if shrinking from the coming ordeal, a by no means uncommon fault, that forward turns, though approached well on the heel, will, in reality, be made on the centre of the blade, the weight being just eased off the back of the skate as the foot whips round; while back turns, which are approached on the centre of the blade, will be made rather more towards the heel, the body having a slight tendency to rock back at the turn if quite upright.

The curve of a skate, if accurately ground, being part of the circumference of a circle of a certain radius, the amount of contact with the ice is the same on whatever portion of the blade the skater is travelling, and it is therefore possible to pivot round on the flat of the blade with equal facility at any point of it, provided the body be upright.

Importance of standing upright

It is not of vital importance, therefore, to determine on what portion of the blade a turn is to be made; what is of vital importance is the perfectly upright position of the body at the moment of the turn. Without this, the skater will never be travelling correctly and easily on the subsequent edge. Indeed, the importance of standing erect in English skating can hardly be exaggerated. The failure to do so is the cause in nine cases out of ten of any difficulty experienced in executing a movement.

Stiffness to be avoided

The upright carriage of the body must not, however, lead to anything like stiffness, an erect position without rigidity being an essential feature of good skating. Even the principle of keeping the employed leg braced, which should not be overlooked, must on the other hand not be exaggerated, since some heel turns are made cleaner and with greater ease if there is a slight, though almost imperceptible, play in the knee just at the turn, this giving a suspicion of life and buoyancy, whereas a too rigidly braced leg, in certain turns, prevents all feeling of elasticity. This is a very different thing to skating with a bent knee, which should, in the English style, be carefully avoided. Complete absence of elasticity, however, is no less a fault, and prevents adaptability to circumstances, while producing an appearance of exaggerated stiffness which is too often conspicuous in English skating, and which not unfrequently prevents an otherwise fine performer from emerging from the category of second class skaters, and taking his place in the first rank.

Having explained at length the principle applying to all turns, supplemented by such general remarks as may be of utility, it will be well here to summarise the whole process.

Summary of phases of preparation for a turn

The preparation for every turn consists, then, of three phases:—

First.—The *hip* on the same side as the rotating arm is *brought forward* (if not the hip of the employed leg, this is effected by forcing back the latter), the *head* being *simultaneously brought round half way*, unless already looking in the direction of the turn.

Second.—The shoulders revolve by pressing back the rotating arm, the hips meanwhile making a strong effort to resist this rotation, while the head follows round after the rotation has commenced, if not already looking in the direction of the turn.

Third.—The tension caused by the contrary rotation of shoulders and hips is relieved by *smartly bringing back the hip* that was forced forward (if not the hip of the employed leg, this is effected by smartly bringing forward the latter), the position of the arms being reversed at the same moment. This results in the whipping round of the foot, and the turn is effected.

In other words, *the preparation for any turn consists of forcing forward the master hip when the rotating arm is the same side as the employed leg; and of forcing back the master hip when the rotating arm is on the other side.*

Approximate time required for preparation

These phases of which the preparation for a turn consists only occupy about three seconds in point of time, unless travelling at high speed, when a longer time is required, and, roughly speaking, should be commenced three or four yards from the spot where the turn is to be effected, a greater distance being required if the turn is approached at high speed, the distance necessarily varying according to the speed of travelling.

English Skating 115

Natural position on edge to be maintained until moment arrives to begin preparation

The skater should be easy and natural, in the correct attitude for the edge he is on, until the moment arrives to prepare for the turn, above all taking care to stand upright, though without anything like stiffness.

The above is applicable to all turns, the amount of rotation in different turns, however, varying according to their nature.

Exact attitude and amount of rotation vary slightly in different skaters

It is useless to attempt to specify with minute accuracy the exact relative positions of travelling foot, hips, and shoulders on any edge, since the semi-sideways position when travelling not only varies according to the edge, but is not absolutely identical in the case of each individual; neither is the amount of revolution possible the same in every case, since this also depends on the build and suppleness of the skater.

Diagrams demonstrating counter movement of hips and shoulders

The following diagrams, however, illustrate sufficiently for practical purposes the principle of the counter movement of hips and shoulders in the two classes of turns, viz., when the rotating arm and master hip are on the same side, and when they are on opposite sides; showing the difference between the attitude when travelling on the edge, at the moment when the foot is ready to whip round, and after the turn; and, in the case of turns where the rotating arm and the master hip are on opposite sides, illustrating the readjustment necessary after the turn in order to assume the correct position for the resulting edge.

1. Rotating arm and master hip on the same side, as in the *C turn* and *B turn* groups.

A. Right hip, the master hip. *B.* Right shoulder, the right arm being the rotating arm.

Right Foot.

1. 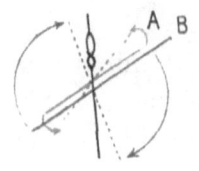 The red and blue lines[47] represent the original position of hips and shoulders respectively. The dotted lines show their position when the foot is ready to whip round.

2.  Position when foot is ready to whip round.

---

[47]In the paperback edition, the figures are reproduced in grayscale. Lowther kindly labeled the red lines "A" and the blue lines "B."

English Skating

3.  Position immediately after turn, being that required for the resulting edge.

In this class of turns no change of position is necessary after the turn is effected, the attitude being correct for the resulting edge.

2. Rotating arm and master hip on opposite sides, as in the *A turn* and *D turn* groups.

A. Right hip, the master hip. *B.* Left shoulder, the left arm being the rotating arm.

Right Foot.

1. 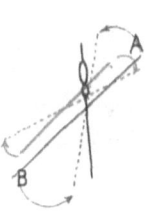 The red and blue lines represent the original position of hips and shoulders respectively. The dotted lines show their position when the foot is ready to whip round.

2. 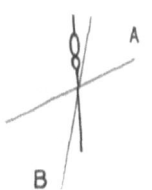 Position when foot is ready to whip round.

3. 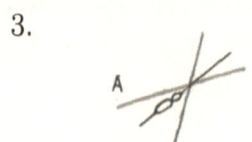 Position immediately after turn, necessitating further revolution of the shoulders, and fresh reversal of the arms.

4.  Result of change indicated, being the correct position for the edge after the turn.

In this class of turns, further revolution of the shoulders, and a second reversal of the arms, this time smooth and deliberate, are necessary after the turn, in order to assume the correct attitude for the resulting edge. If this is a back edge, the head also has to be brought round.

The above illustrates the principle of the "hip *versus* shoulder" system, which should be applied to all turns in the degree admitted by the individual capacity of the skater.

Mohawks and Choctaws

The same principles hold good in the preparation for *Mohawks* and *Choctaws*, every two-footed movement having its analogous turn, and *vice versâ*.

The Outside Mohawk may be regarded as a two-footed bracket; the Outside Choctaw as a two-footed counter; while the Inside Mohawk may be regarded as a two-footed *A* turn, and the Inside Choctaw as a two-footed inside rocker, the preparation in each case being the same as for the analogous turn. As, however, it is better to learn to skate the two-footed movements first, the manner of skating Mohawks and Choctaws should rather be considered as a guide for the analogous turns than the latter as a guide for the analogous two-footed movements.

The method of skating *Mohawks* and *Choctaws*, therefore, is as follows: The hip of the unemployed leg is brought forward by forcing back the master hip, and the hips then resist the rotation of the shoulders till the tension is relieved by putting down the unemployed foot, which should be allowed to get hold of the ice first with the inside of the toe, a shove being obtained with the other foot as it leaves the ice, and the arms being reversed at the same time. The unemployed foot must, of course, be sufficiently turned out at the last moment to enable the skater to get hold of the ice with the toe of the skate. The change of foot for the back edge obviates the necessity of any subsequent alteration in the position of shoulders and arms, as is necessary in order to be in the correct attitude for the resulting edge in skating the analogous turns.

In the case of the privileged few who can naturally spread-eagle their feet, it is merely necessary to put down the unemployed foot on the proper back edge, so that the feet are heel to heel as the other foot is lifted from the ice. No impetus, however, is gained by the change of feet, as there is nothing in the nature of a stroke. What is gained in facility, therefore, is lost in power.

Special remarks on the different groups of turns

Although the same broad principle applies to all turns, a few special remarks are applicable to each separate group. Every turn, as already stated, has its analogous two-footed movement, facility in skating which is of great assistance in learning the turns. As, however, the analogous two-footed movements in the case of the C and B turn groups consist of Cross-Mohawks and Cross-Choctaws, which are hardly ever skated, it is in reality only in learning the A and D turn groups that this help is available. We will, therefore, deal with the latter groups first.

A turn group

In skating

		(Analogous two-footed movement)
The	A turn	(Inside Mohawk)
	I F rocker	(Inside Choctaw)
	O F counter	(Choctaw)
and	O F bracket	(Mohawk)

the moment to make the turn is the moment when, in skating the analogous two-footed movement, the other foot would be put down, the preparation being exactly as for the corresponding Mohawk or Choctaw, except as regards the turning out of the unemployed foot, which is unnecessary. Care must be taken to approach these turns *well on the heel*, and in the case of the O F counter and bracket, at the last moment, while so travelling, to endeavour to turn out the toe of the employed foot, which results in a slight accentuation of the curve. This facilitates the turn and counteracts the tendency to change the edge. In the case of the O F counter and bracket, the forward hip must be very smartly brought back at the turn, which is effected by bringing forward the hip of the employed leg, this being the master hip.

D turn group

Similarly in skating

		(Analogous two-footed movement)
The	D turn	(O B and O F)
	O B rocker	(O B and I F)
	I B counter	(I B and O F)
and	I B bracket	(I B and I F)

the moment to make the turn is the moment when it would be convenient to put down the other foot in skating the analogous two-footed movement.

In skating the latter group of turns care must be taken not to get too hard on the edge after the turn. The head should remain stationary till the shoulders have begun to rotate, and should not at the turn be brought too far round in the direction of rotation, this having a tendency to throw the skater hard on the resulting edge in the case of the D turn and I B counter, and to prevent his holding the resulting edge in the case of the O B rocker and I B bracket. For the same reason, the principle of smartly bringing back the hip which was brought forward during the preparation for the turn must be considerably modified, since the sudden shifting of the hips has the same tendency. If control of the edge after any turn is lost, so that there is danger of involuntarily making another turn with the same rotation, the remedy is to go through the preparation for a counter till control of the edge has been regained.

In skating the I B counter and bracket, while travelling on the back edge, an endeavour should be made at the last moment to turn in the heel of the employed foot, which results in a slight accentuation of the curve and counteracts the tendency to change the edge.

An O F bracket has been aptly described as a "one-footed Mohawk," and a D turn might on the same principle be described as a "one-footed O B and O F," and so on, to convey an idea of the analogy between the turns and the corresponding two-footed movements. Facility in skating the latter is therefore of great assistance when beginning to learn these turns, which, conversely, when the skater is familiar with them, serve as a guide for the corresponding two-footed movements, since in skating these the body should go through exactly the same preparation before the unemployed foot takes up the fresh edge.

C turn group

The other turns have likewise, as already stated, their analogous two-footed movements, but which are not commonly skated, and therefore of little practical use as a guide.

		(Analogous two-footed movement)
The	C turn	(Forward cross Mohawk)
	O F rocker	(Forward cross Choctaw)
	I F counter	(Inside cross Choctaw)
and	I F bracket	(Inside cross Mohawk)

are the easiest group of turns, the maximum amount of rotation not being necessary, while the head hardly alters its position. It is this facility of preparation that commends them to the beginner, in spite of no preliminary practice of simple two-footed movements being available in the case of the A turn and D turn groups. Similarly, the comparatively small amount of preparation required renders the D turn group the easiest of the back turns; the position, however, immediately after the turn, is incorrect for the resulting edge, in the case of the latter, and has to be rectified as previously explained.

The comparative ease with which the turn is effected in the C turn and D turn groups is to a great extent due to the fact that the foot is shifted, toe or heel as the case may be, towards the inside, *i.e.*, across the body, and not outwards as in the case of the A turn and B turn groups; thus—

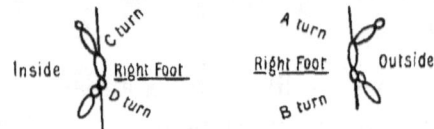

In skating the I F counter and bracket, while travelling well on the heel, an endeavour should be made at the last moment to turn in the toe of the employed foot, which results in a slightly accentuation of the curve, and counteracts the tendency to change the edge.

B turn group

		(Analogous two-footed movement)
The	B turn	(Back inside cross Mohawk)
	I B rocker	(Back inside cross Choctaw)
	O B counter	(Back cross Choctaw)
and	O B bracket	(Back cross Mohawk)

are the most difficult group of turns, since they require the most preparation, the head having to be brought round till it is looking over the other shoulder, while the shoulders themselves have to rotate to the maximum possible extent, it being more imperatively necessary than in other turns that they should be approximately in the same straight line as the travelling foot before the turn is effected. The three different phases of preparation, therefore, must be more conscientiously put into practice for this group than is absolutely necessary in the case of other turns. There is a special, and almost universal, tendency to lean forward when approaching these turns, as if shrinking from the coming ordeal, whereas this group more than any other demands a very erect position at the turn. The old familiar injunction, "feel the back of your collar," is as good a corrective as any other, implying an upright carriage of the head which is incompatible with stooping forward. "Feel tall at the turn" is an expression that seems in some cases to bring home to the beginner the meaning of what is required when all other advice fails.

In the case of the *B turn* and *I B rocker*, the skater will find it of assistance to bring the heel of the travelling foot well in under him before the turn, but without anything like a twitch to mar the smoothness of the movement, unless it be in an emergency, when the turn can be rapidly executed by *suddenly* turning in the heel of the travelling foot, thus accentuating the curve, and getting a good grip of the ice with the heel preparatory to flicking the foot round. The latter method, however, should only be resorted to as a makeshift to save the situation, when for any reason a B turn has to be made at short notice. In skating a *B turn*, it may further be remarked, the foot should not be brought too far round at the turn, as the slightly strained feeling on the O F edge, which is confessed to by even the very best skaters, is more noticeable when the cusp is very open. When skating the *I B rocker*, on the other hand, the foot should be brought round as far as possible, as in the case of all rockers.

In the case of the *O B counter* and *bracket*, it should be noted that a very sideways position on the O B edge, before preparing for the turn, facilitates the movement, the object being to force back the hip of the unemployed leg as far as possible; while shifting the weight for a moment on to the front part of the skate, though without lurching forward, as the shoulders begin to revolve, rectifies the balance, and prevents a strained feeling in the new position. The weight must, however, be immediately shifted back as soon as this is achieved. At the last moment, before the turn is effected, the skater should make an effort to turn the heel of the travelling foot *outwards*, which has the effect of slightly accentuating the curve, instead of bringing it in under him, as in the B turn. This corrects the tendency to change the edge.

The O B counter has been graphically described as "a B turn, only more so," which conveys a very fair idea of its nature.

Position of unemployed foot in "hip v. shoulder" system

It may be noted that in skating the *A turn and D turn groups* the result of bringing forward the hip of the unemployed leg is that the unemployed foot is slightly further forward, and slightly more turned in, than in skating the C turn and B turn groups. In the *C turn and B turn groups* the bringing forward of the hip of the employed leg has the contrary effect, the unemployed leg being carried well behind, with the toe rather more turned out. When the turns are made on the old principle of bringing shoulders and hips round together, the opposite is the case, since the action of the hips is exactly the converse.

Remarks applicable to certain classes of turns irrespectively of group to which they belong

One or two features in connection with rockers, counters, and brackets, irrespective of the group they belong to, should be noticed:—

Rockers and brackets

In skating all *rockers and brackets* the farther the foot is turned round—that is, the larger the angle of the cusp—the easier it is to hold to the resulting edge. The failure to turn the foot sufficiently round in the case of brackets sometimes results in a counter followed by a change of edge, instead of the *bonâ fide* movement. An apparent bit of serpentine after the turn will be seen, just as in the case of the rocker, whether the bracket is *bonâ fide* or not, but the skater himself will be conscious of the difference between the two.

Counters and brackets

In all *counters and brackets* the forcing of the toe out or in, according to the edge, for the forward turns, the heel out or in, according to the edge, for the back turns, at the last moment, as previously described, is of considerable importance. This results in a slight accentuation of the curve, and counteracts the tendency to change the edge.

Hints with regard to special combinations

The following hints with regard to special combinations may be of use to beginners:—

Two turns to a centre

In skating two turns, whether outside or inside turns, to a centre, the moment to make the second turn is as soon as the centre is visible over the shoulder, while preparing in the correct manner for the turn in question, the centre being allowed to come in sight without straining to see it. The common fault is that of making the turn before the centre comes in view, and consequently too far away from it.

Three turns to a centre

In skating three turns to a centre, the second turn should be made half way round the circle, and the skater should not be increasing his distance from the centre during the whole of the second curve. By keeping the eye on the centre, and not turning the head round too soon in preparation for the second turn, it is easy to judge the exact moment for making it. Another method, however, is recommended in the case of beginners, which will enable them to prepare for the second turn with greater deliberation, viz., to make the second turn as soon as it is *possible* to catch sight of the centre over the shoulder, which is naturally before it comes in view without striving to see it, as in skating two turns to a centre.

Back two turns with cross-roll

In skating back two turns with the cross-roll, in order to keep the curves large and on a light edge, the head should be kept in the same position the whole time, facing throughout over the shoulder corresponding to the employed leg, instead of being brought round into the correct position for the D turn. As sideways an attitude as possible should be adopted, and the skater should be careful never to get hard on the edge.

Whenever there is any special reason for keeping lightly on the I F edge after a D turn, or I B counter, it is better not to look round in the direction of the turn.

The general rules as to the proper position for the head for each edge must not be too slavishly adhered to. Such rules are merely intended to facilitate the movement, and when a slight deviation from them is found better to serve this end, their too strict observance would defeat the very object they have in view.

The value of this movement as practice, if skated with fairly large curves of a uniform size, consists in the necessity of checking the rotation which even many experienced skaters find some difficulty in controlling. Provided the rotation set up is not allowed to dictate the moment for making the turns, but each turn is postponed till the skater intends to make it, no movement provides finer practice in obtaining mastery over the skate. If the rotation, on the other hand, is allowed to spin the body round like a teetotum, so that two turns with small curves on a hard edge are involuntarily made, it is worthless as practice, and it is the inability, in many cases, to prevent this that results in its condemnation as a stupid cramped movement. It is precisely this tendency to be run away with by the skate that has to be overcome, and which makes the complete mastery over this movement one of the necessary links in a skater's education. Where this tendency is very pronounced, the cause, through rarely admitted, is, in nearly all cases, inability to skate the back cross-roll properly, resulting in loss of control over the back edge. "Be sure your sins will find you out" is here exemplified. Neglect of one movement is punished by unnecessary difficulty in another. However fine a performer the skater may otherwise be, unless he acquires complete mastery over this particular, and much abused, movement, there is a serious gap in his skating education.

O B counters and brackets at centre

In skating O B counters and brackets, when the turn has to be made at the centre, the preparation for the turn should not be begun till the centre can be seen over the shoulder corresponding to the unemployed leg, and the skater is, roughly speaking, about three or four yards from it, the distance varying according to the speed of travelling. Care should be taken when beginning to revolve the shoulders to shift the weight momentarily to the front part of the skate, in the manner previously explained. The preparation for the turn being made as already prescribed, allowance must be made for the accentuation of the curve, which to a certain extent is admissable, and even necessary, a slight draw back resulting from the effort to turn out the heel just before the turn is effected; but care must be taken to keep on a light edge to avoid the tendency to exaggerate this accentuation of the curve, and make a swung turn in the Continental style. By skating straight *at* the centre up to the moment when the head is turned away from it, it will be found that the turn will be made on the near side of the orange at about the correct distance from it, the curve at the last moment as the draw back is made swerving slightly to the inside of the true direction of the original edge.

The common faults are—beginning to prepare for the turn too far from the centre, which necessitates remaining in a strained position too long, during which the centre is invisible; failing to make allowance for the slightly altered direction of the curve as the turn is approached, and not being sufficiently erect at the moment of turning.

O F bracket and B turn to a centre

An O F bracket followed by a B turn to a centre is a combination which is generally found difficult. This is usually because the bracket turn is made too soon, in which case the resulting edge takes the skater straight out from the centre, necessitating a disproportionately long back edge before circling in sufficiently to make the B turn within a reasonable distance of the centre, or a longer edge of O F after the B turn than is compatible with arriving at the centre with sufficient pace. The skater should start as though about to make a forward entire,[48] and postpone the bracket turn till half way round the circle, that is to say, he should not make the turn until a continuation of the original curve would begin to bring him in towards the centre. The bracket turn will result in his receding rather further from the centre before circling in towards it, affording time to prepare for the B turn, which should not be made till the centre is visible over the shoulder corresponding to the employed leg.

A bracket entire is skated on the same principle, the tail being held till the centre is reached.

Bracket, or counter, after a B turn

A bracket, or counter, after a B turn is another combination presenting some difficulty to the beginner, the reason being that, after the B turn, the original rotation has to be checked and reversed. To effect this it is necessary to prepare deliberately for the turn, on the principles already explained, before attempting to make it.

Turns in general to a centre

In skating any turn to a centre in combined figure skating, the skater should be travelling towards the centre easily and naturally, in the correct attitude for the edge he is on, till within three or four yards of it, the distance varying according to the speed, it being unnecessary to

---

[48] A circle on a forward outside edge. See page 81.

begin to prepare for the turn sooner. It is only when making turns at high speed that a longer preparation is necessary.

Recapitulation

In order to skate any turn, *hips* and *shoulders* must *work against one another*, the hip play being by far the most important factor in every case.

First.—The *hip* on the same side as the rotating arm is *brought forward* (if not the hip of the employed leg, this is effected by forcing back the latter, which is the master hip), the *head*, if not already looking in the direction of the turn, being *simultaneously brought round half way*.

Second.—The shoulders revolve by pressing back the rotating arm, the *hips* meanwhile making a *strong effort to resist this rotation*, while the head follows round after the rotation has commenced, unless already looking in the direction of the turn.

Third.—The tension caused by the contrary rotation of shoulders and hips is relieved by *smartly bringing back the hip that was forced forward* (if not the hip of the employed leg, this is effected by smartly bringing forward the latter, which is the master hip), the position of the arms being reversed at the same moment, a movement which should, however, though smartly executed, be as far as possible disguised.

This results in the whipping round of the foot, and the turn is effected.

In other words, *the preparation for any turn consists of forcing the master hip forward when the rotating arm is the same side as the employed leg, and of forcing the master hip back when the rotating arm is on the other side.*

When the rotating arm and the master hip are the same side, the attitude is correct for the resulting edge when the foot whips round; when the rotating arm is the opposite side to the master hip, a readjustment of position is necessary after the turn. (See pages 116 and 117.)

The whole process only occupies about three seconds, unless travelling at high speed, when a longer time is advisable, and, roughly speaking, should be commenced about three or four yards from the spot where the turn is to be made, the distance varying according to the speed of travelling.

All forward turns should be approached *hard on the heel.*

All back turns should be approached on the *centre of the blade.*

The skater should at all times stand erect, drawing himself up to his full height at every turn, and as far as possible avoid looking down.

Concluding remarks

The skater should aim at travelling noiselessly and lightly, stealing smoothly over the ice without jar or unnecessary friction. He should never skate, so to speak, as if he were a dead weight, but while in motion he should always have a certain feeling of elasticity.

In practising turns beginners should avoid the too common habit of starting off with a rush, in their anxiety for speed and power. This method merely leads to a rough, scrambling performance, and is quite useless as preliminary training for combined figure skating, where no movement can be made under similar conditions, but each portion of the figure must be taken up at once with a single stroke from the previous edge.

Power to be acquired by correct striking, and not by preliminary rush

The only useful method of practising turns, with a view to combined figure skating, is to endeavour by correct striking, on which alone powerful and steady skating depends, to acquire the necessary speed for the movement to be skated. The necessity for correct striking is, in general, not sufficiently realised, and those who have accustomed themselves during practice alone to depend on a rush for their initial impetus are too apt to neglect this elementary, but wholly indispensable acquirement, with the result that, when taking part in a combined figure, they find their large, bold curves reduced to exceedingly modest dimension, and their balance to often incorrect on taking up a fresh edge.

Large turns made at sufficiently high speed to necessitate a preliminary rush are, no doubt, a test of fine skating, but should not be too much indulged in till the skater is a really accomplished performer.

Caution to beginners not to skate beyond their strength

A beginner, then, should beware of trying to skate beyond his strength. Power, which should, of course, be ultimately aimed at, must be acquired by degrees. To endeavour to force it merely results in a rough, scrambling performance, scraped turns, and a general want of steadiness. He should always skate within himself, that is, just as powerfully as he can consistently with good skating, and not be led away by the popular fallacy that size and speed necessarily imply the latter, or seek for the applause which these qualities, in spite of all defects of skating, never fail to elicit from the ignorant.

The desire to skate big and bold is in itself most laudable, but this caution to beginners not to sacrifice everything to size is necessary, since this is beginning at the wrong end. Size and power will come imperceptibly as their general skating improves, and their principal care should be never to skate any movement in a rough, slovenly manner. "Take care of the form and the power will take care of itself" should be the beginner's motto, as power depends on correct striking, correct carriage of the body, and clean turns, none of which are probably if the skater is making a lunging effort to achieve what is beyond his strength; while "*ars est celare artem*"[49] should be the motto of the experienced skater, necessitating the same qualities in a still higher degree, by which alone all visible effort can be eliminated from difficult movements.

---

[49] "It is art to conceal art."

The cover of Henry C. Lowther's *Combined Figure-Skating* (London: Horace Cox, 1902).

Preface

The following treatise is a sequel to the two former ones intended to serve as preliminary preparation previous to studying the subject of combined figure-skating, entitled, respectively, "Edges and Striking," and "Principle of Skating Turns." The three together form a complete treatise on English skating.

It is hoped that the portability of the present volume may commend it to those who desire a book of reference on the ice. Diagrams of elementary figures[50] for practice are given for the guidance of beginners, and a few really difficult sets for advanced skaters are appended.

The subject of hand-in-hand skating, which is briefly dealt with, is only touched on owing to the possible use of this style in combined figure-skating.

Appendix II. on the "Care of Rinks" has been added at the suggestion of Mr. Carl de Bary, whose experience in connection with the making and preservation of rinks in the Engadine, and elsewhere, entitles him to speak with authority. The substance of the counsel given is his, though not the words. Owing to his energy and thorough knowledge of the subject, enthusiasts are enabled to enjoy skating at St. Moritz for a considerable time after the rinks, but for him, would be

---

[50]These are combined figures, meant to be watched while the skaters do them, not the now-better-known compulsory and special figures, meant to be drawn on the ice and inspected after the skater has finished.

abandoned to their fate. The credentials, which guarantee the value of his counsel, consist of the successful production of ice fit to skate on, under adverse circumstances, when others have given up the task as hopeless.

HENRY C. LOWTHER

Combined figure-skating

Combined figure-skating consists of two or more persons skating the same movements together starting from a given centre (usually an orange), in the different directions required to make the figure symmetrical, and performing evolutions round, returning to, and receding from, the centre at the same time, according to the nature of the call.

Various styles of combined figure-skating

1. Skating in pairs, crossing at the centre

When an *even* number of skaters take part in the figure, it is better to skate in pairs, each skater being opposite his partner with the centre exactly between them. The first pair must make each movement a second before the next pair, and the second pair before the third pair, if there are more than four skaters, which is the usual number, so that they may arrive at the centre one pair at a time, and be able to pass it on their respective sides, before the next pair come up, since the latter have to cut in between them from opposite directions and cross their tracks. We will suppose four persons about to take part in the figure.

How to leave centre. The skaters place themselves symmetrically in pairs, that is, at the four points of the compass, each being opposite his partner, with the

A combined figure: "Twice back centre-change entire." From Montagu S. Monier-Williams, Winter Randell Pidgeon, and Arthur Dryden, *Figure Skating, Simple and Combined* (London: Macmillan & Co., 1892), frontispiece.

centre between them, and at a distance of about twelve feet from it. The caller[51] and his partner start first, skate up to the centre by means of a single stroke of outside edge on the left foot, and begin the movement called on the right foot, each keeping the centre to the inside of the first curve of the figure. This is called the *off side*. Hence, if the movement begins on the outside edge of the right foot, each skater strikes off on what is to be the left side of the centre; if the movement begins on the inside edge of the right foot, on the right side, thus:

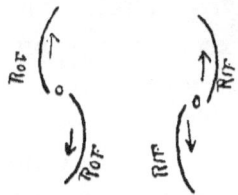

This is the general rule for leaving the centre on commencing a figure from rest; but it does not follow that on returning to the centre it will be again left in the same manner. This rests with the caller, and the other skaters must be prepared to follow his lead.

As soon as the first pair are clear of the centre, the next pair start off in the same manner, cutting in between them and crossing their tracks.

Care must be taken to strike off in the proper direction. Care must be taken when striking off at

---

[51]In combined skating, as in some types of folk dancing, the caller is the person responsible for announcing the next maneuver.

the centre to do so in the proper direction, that is, the tendency to strike off too much to the right or left, according to the edge, must be avoided.

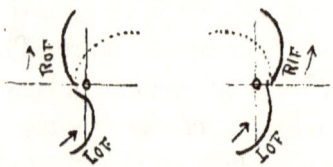

The dotted lines show the wrong tendency to be avoided.

How to approach centre. The rule for approaching the centre is exactly the reverse, since, unless the caller gives special directions, the centre must always be kept to the *outside* of the curve being skated. This is called the *near side*, and the centre should always be so approached, unless the word 'off' is introduced into the call, in which case it must be kept to the *inside* of the curve, thus:

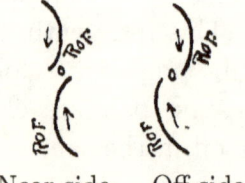

Near side.　Off side.

Diagrams illustrating how to pairs leave and approach the centre. The following diagrams illustrate the method of leaving and approaching the centre when two pairs are skating.

Only one pair, of course, must be at the centre at a time, the next pair cutting in between and across their tracks, as soon as there is room for them to do so.

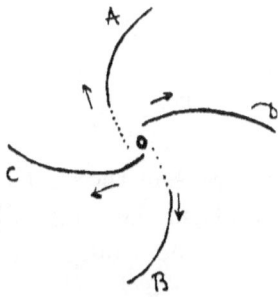

Method of leaving centre R O F or L I F.

The dotted lines represent the distance travelled by the first pair, A. and B., before the second pair, D. and C., leave the centre, *i.e.*, about 6ft.

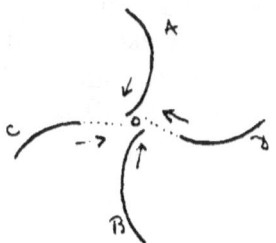

Method of approaching centre on *near side* R O F or R I B; L I F or L O B.

The dotted lines represent the distance the second pair, C. and D, should be from the centre when the first pair, A. and B., reach it, *i.e.*, about 6ft.

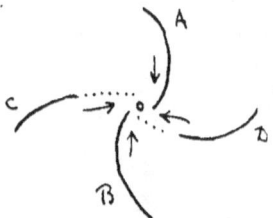

Method of approaching centre on *off side* R O F or R I B; L I F or L O B.

The dotted lines represent the distance the second pair C., and D., should be from the centre when the first pair, A. and B., reach it, *i.e.*, about 6ft.

Special duties of first and second pair respectively. When skating in pairs, and crossing at the centre, the special duty of the caller's partner is to keep the centre exactly between the caller and himself, the two making their turns and changes of edge as nearly as possible simultaneously. The second pair should pay more attention to keeping exactly half way between the first pair, on their respective sides of the centre, than to one another's skating, making their turns and changes of edge just after the first pair.

How to avoid collisions at centre when more than two pairs are skating. If more than four persons are taking part in the figure, and all are in the vicinity of the centre, some leaving, and others approaching it, in order to avoid collisions and prevent confusion, it should be borne in mind that those leaving the centre must give way to those approaching it—that is, they should always pass to the outside of the curve of the skater on his way to the centre, and never cut across him.

2. Simultaneous skating

When the skaters are *uneven* in number, what is known as "simultaneous skating" is more satisfactory than skating in pairs, otherwise one skater is obliged to perform alone without a partner opposite him, which gives the set a lopsided appearance.

Each skater has his own separate imaginary centre. Common centre never approached. In this style of skating the performers must be equidistant, and each must skate to an imaginary centre of his own on the circumference of a circle drawn round the common centre at a distance of two, three, or more feet, the size of the circle varying according to the number of skaters. No skater must ever cross the circumference of this circle, but swerve to the right or left according to the requirements of the figure just before touching it.

Skaters never cross one another's tracks. Thus the skaters never cross one another at a common centre, there being as many centres as there are skaters, at equal distances round the circumference of the circle drawn round the orange. Each skater on arriving at his own imaginary centre follows in the tracks of his right or left-hand neighbour, as the case may be, every movement throughout the figure being made simultaneously by all.

An even number of skaters can equally well adopt this style of skating, which is the most effective to look at, since all make their movements simultaneously; but skating in pairs is better practice, and more interesting, from the greater accuracy which it necessitates.

Same rules apply as to leaving and approaching different centres. The same rules apply in simultaneous skating as to the side on which the centres should be left and approached, the only difference being that no two skaters have the same centre, neither do they cross one another's tracks. We will suppose five people about to take part in the figure. Here, then, there will be five imaginary centres. These, however, are not fixed points, but keep shifting round to meet the requirements of the figure, each skater's imaginary centre always being the point on the circumference of the circle exactly half way between his right and left-hand neighbour.

Diagrams illustrating method of approaching and leaving centres in simultaneous skating. The following diagrams illustrate the method of leaving and approaching the centres in simultaneous skating.

English Skating 153

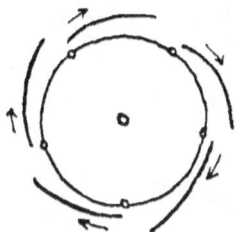

Direction in which different skaters would start from the imaginary centres on commencing figure on R O F or L I F.

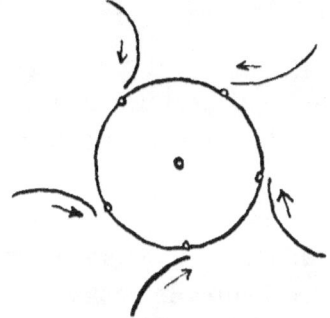

Method of approaching centres on *near side* R O F or R I B; L I F or L O B.

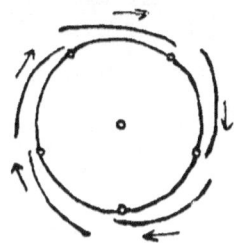

Method of approaching centres on *off side* R O F or R I B; L I F or L O B.

The following diagram illustrates the deviation of the curve necessary when approaching on the near side, as compared with the curve required when approaching on the off side.

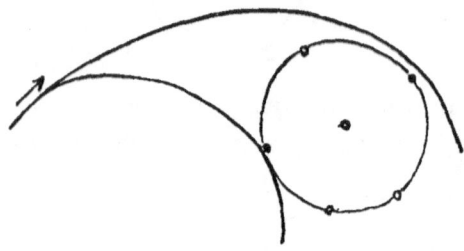

Great importance of understanding correct manner of leaving and approaching centre. The manner of leaving and approaching the centre is the most important feature in combined figure-skating, and must be thoroughly understood before attempting to take part in a combined figure. It must be impressed on the beginner that the "*near side*" is the side where the centre is to the *outside* of the curve skated, and that the "*off side*" is the side where the centre is to the *inside* of the curve skated; that, starting from rest, a figure is always commenced on the *off side*, and that the centre is always approached on the *near side*, if no directions to the contrary are given by the caller.

3. Circling in opposite directions

Another variety of combined figure-skating, which is, however, seldom made use of, consists of two pairs circling in opposite directions. To effect this, the second pair start off on the opposite foot to the first pair, and skate on a slightly smaller circumference, thus, always, when meeting one of the other pair travelling in the opposite direction, passing him on the inside, that is, between him and the centre. The only object of skating in this way is to enable two comparatively weak skaters to take part in a combined figure with two powerful skaters, without obliging the latter to skate down to them. This method is sometimes useful when the set of composed of two men and two ladies. *Cæteris paribus*, the men are naturally capable of skating rather bigger, and should therefore skate together and start first, the ladies following and commencing on the other foot, thus circling in the opposite direction as described.

4. *Skating hand-in-hand to a centre*

One other method of combined figure-skating, which is at present rather a possibility of the future than a recognized style, may be noticed. This consists in a development of hand-in-hand skating, eight performers, skating two and two in this manner, taking part in the figure, instead of four skating alone. All figures made use of in combined figure-skating can be skated hand-in-hand, as scuds, and it is therefore possible for four couples to skate them thus to a centre. Many ladies who are not sufficiently steady and accurate when skating alone could in this manner take part in a set, if piloted by a really good skater, and for this reason alone the hand-in-hand style is worth cultivating for purposes of combined figure-skating.

Terms used in combined figure-skating

It now remains to explain the various terms used in combined figure-skating:

A *movement* consists of any combination of edges and turns, skated on one foot without putting the other down, *e.g.*, a three, or Q.[52]

A *figure* may consist of one or more movements, with a distinctive name. Therefore, a three, or Q, are also figures. Once back, Mohawk, Choctaw, &c., are figures consisting of more than one movement.

A *call* is a combination of movements or figures starting from, and ending at, the centre, which may, however, be passed more than once during the call.

A *set* consists of a series of calls continuing till a dismiss call is given.

When the centre has to be passed during a call, the manner of approaching and passing it is indicated by the words *meet, pass, centre,* or, *off meet, off pass, off centre.*

Meet, off meet

Means that the skaters have to come up to the centre, on the near or off side, as the case may be, and begin the succeeding movement at the centre.

---

[52] A change of edge followed by a turn. See page 96.

Pass, off pass

Means that the centre must be approached and passed, on the near or off side, as the case may be, before taking up the next movement.

Centre, off centre

Means that the movement so defined has to be executed at the centre, on the near or off side, as the case may be; thus "centre turn" means a turn made at the centre on the near side; "off centre Mohawk" means that the back edge of the Mohawk is taken up at the centre on the off side, and so on.

Entire, entire off

Means that the movement to which the term is applied finishes at the centre, on the near or off side, as the case may be. It is only used in connection with movements commencing at the centre, or during which the centre is passed.

About means that the direction of circling round the centre is reversed. If the centre is to the inside of the curve being skated this is effected by curling in between the centre and the circumference, the curve being held till the skater is beginning to again recede from the centre. If the centre is to the outside of the curve being skated, and the skater therefore receding from it, he must continue circling on the same curve till its continuation would begin to bring him in towards the centre. The word "about" is used immediately after the movement to be so skated. Hence "Forward three about" means that the tail of the three has to be brought about, whereas "Forward about three" means that the about movement precedes the turn.

About, about, is a further development of the above, the curve being held till the original point of departure is returned to, a whole circle being thus made.

Out and in means that the skater should recede from and return to the centre, instead of circling round it. Figures of this class are known as "boomerangs."

The following diagrams illustrate the above definitions:

English Skating

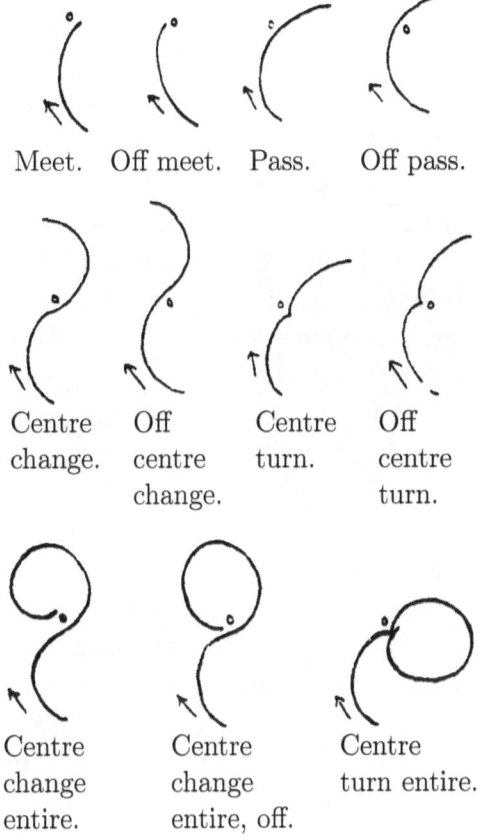

Meet.   Off meet.   Pass.   Off pass.

Centre change.   Off centre change.   Centre turn.   Off centre turn.

Centre change entire.   Centre change entire, off.   Centre turn entire.

A change of foot is denoted by the word "*and*" emphasised. In certain figures, however, with a recognized name, it is omitted, since, knowing the figure, the skaters are aware that a change of foot is necessary. These figures are the following:

Mohawks and Choctaws

Once (twice) back, i.e., a forward three (C turn) followed by an O B on the other foot. This is repeated if twice back is called.

Inside once (twice) back, i.e., an I F three (A turn) followed by an I B on the other foot. This is repeated if inside twice back is called.

Once (twice) forward, i.e., an O B three (D turn) followed by an O F on the other foot. This is repeated if twice forward is called, necessitating a Mohawk to get on to the O B edge.

Inside once (twice) forward, i.e., an I B three (B turn) followed by an I F on the other foot. This is repeated if inside twice forward is called, necessitating an inside Mohawk to get on to the I B edge.

These figures are occasionally varied by substituting some other turn which must be specified in the call, thus: "once bracket back," "twice inside bracket back," "once counter back," &c., the edge is taken up by the other foot continuing in the direction of the curve succeeding the turn; except in the case of the somewhat unusual calls "Once (twice) reverse back," "Inside once (twice) reverse forward," &c., which take the skater straight out from the centre. The general and clearer method of calling these figures is "Forward three and I B," and "I B turn and O F," the latter necessitating a Choctaw to get on to the I B edge, if the movement has to be repeated. And similarly in the case of all such figures. The occasional practice, however, of calling them in the former manner makes it necessary for the skater to understand the meaning of the word "reverse." It is furthermore unnecessary to use the word "*and*" on returning to the centre at the end of a call, to indicate a change of feet.

A *dismiss call* is the conclusion of a set, the final curve receding from, instead of approaching, the centre. It is customary for each skater to salute his partner as he sails away into space, for which reason the final curve should be an I B edge, otherwise the skaters would be unable to face one another.

Manner of circling round the centre

It is now necessary to explain the manner of circling round the centre, and how the various movements of a figure are mapped out so as to return to the centre at the end of the call.

The imaginary circle, of which the orange is the centre, is supposed to be divided into four equal segments by imaginary lines radiating from the centre, and certain portions of the call have to be skated within certain defined limits. There is, however, a diversity of practice as regards the limits of the circumference, and the amount of circling to be done.

Diversity of practice

Some uphold the principle of circling round the centre to a far greater extent than others, and when skating "twice back" reach the limit of their circumference for circling purposes on the first back, the first back occupying one quarter of the circle, the second completing the half circle; nor do they admit the principle of flattening any curve of the figure with a view to arriving more directly at their objective, but almost make a spiral of the final curve, allowing it eventually to curl into the centre. This style is generally characterised by want of space, with a tendency to get too hard on the edge, resulting in too much rotation.

Those who take the *extreme* opposite view can hardly be said to circle round the centre at all, as when skating "twice back" their object is to get as far out into the country as possible, and return as direct to the centre as the nature of the figure admits of, thus, more or less, making all figures of the boomerang type.

If the movement following the "twice back" is intended to bring them to the centre, they begin to turn in towards it on the second back, as if "back about" were to be skated, before commencing it, and then run in as straight as possible.

This style of combined figure-skating, which is a somewhat new departure, but which has a certain number of enthusiastic advocates, has the serious drawback of necessitating more space than is usually available, even on an empty rink. In view of the ever-increasing number of skaters without a corresponding increase of skating accommodation, a style which practically involves the monopoly of a rink by four skaters is foredoomed, even were it generally admitted to be superior to all others. This consideration must in the long run outweigh individual preference. Skaters who advocate this style generally have a tendency to exaggerate the light edge, and to execute every movement almost on the flat of the blade. Indeed, their turns are often merely a cusp in the middle of a straight line, thus ─────⋏─────, and it is only by bearing in mind the trend of the original curve, and waiting to see the eventual direction taken, that it is possible to decide whether the turn were intended for a simple turn, a rocker, a bracket, or a counter.

Turns thus made after a prolonged run on the flat of the skate, to be followed by a corresponding straight line after, can hardly be regarded as *bonâ fide*. Such skaters aim principally at size and speed, but unless these qualities can be combined with *bonâ fide* turns, that is, a true edge right up to the turn and immediately after (the skater only being on the flat of the blade at the very moment of changing the direction from forwards to backwards or *vice-versâ*), however bold, and however faultless in other respects, the performance cannot be regarded as above criticism.

Diagrams illustrating two extreme methods

The following diagrams illustrate the two extremes in skating "twice back."

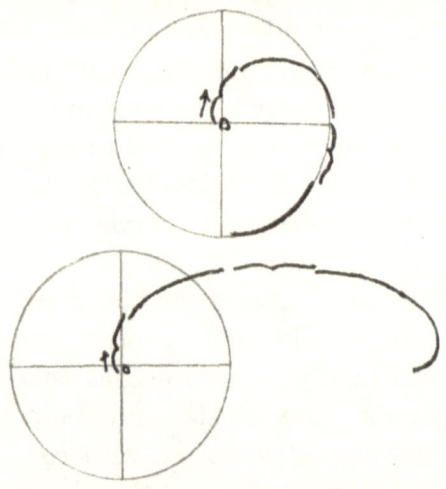

The extreme of either style, therefore, is likely to lead to certain defects of skating, except in the case of a very limited number of exceptionally fine skaters, whose skill is sufficient to counteract harmful tendencies. If, however, anything like a universally recognised style is to be arrived at, it must be such as is productive of the best results among the generality of figure-skaters.

In the absence of such it is clearly necessary to have a definite understanding when taking part in a figure as to the amount of circling to be done, and the manner of skating the last part of the call, in order to keep square. The caller should observe uniformity of practice in this respect, since, without knowing his intention beforehand, the skaters would experience some difficulty in adapting their skating to his.

Compromise recommended

On the whole it would appear that the old adage "in medio tutissimus ibis"[53] here holds good, and that the most satisfactory result is obtained by avoiding either extreme—that is, the skaters should, though circling round the centre, be slightly increasing their distance from it till the completion of the second back, which should bring them half way round the circle. Thus:

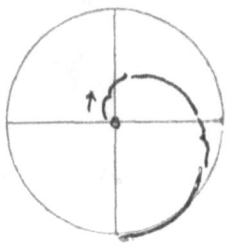

The object of the figure "twice back" being to obtain more speed than can be acquired with "once back," the skaters should be travelling faster on repeating the movement, and consequently require more space. As, then, the first back is supposed to occupy one quarter, and the second to complete the half of the circle, in order not to exceed this half circle limit it is necessary to continue increasing the distance from the centre till the completion of the second back, otherwise the following movement will have to be taken up hurriedly, before the previous one is fairly skated out.

Regarding the furthest point reached on the second back, which in the case of fairly powerful skaters should be about fifty feet from the centre, as the limit

---

[53]"You will go most safely by the middle course."

of their circumference, the skaters should then continue to circle round the centre, and give the proper value to each part of the movement till the *final curve* is begun, which alone should be flattened so as to cut straight for the centre. This enables the centre to be reached with more pace than if the circling were continued to the last, without prejudice to the figure as a whole by a too free use of the flat of the blade throughout the movement, since, as above stated, the tendency resulting from the system of reducing circling to a minimum is to unduly exaggerate the light edge, the skater travelling practically in a straight line before and after each turn. There should be an understanding also as to the manner of taking up the I B edge after a previous back edge. The difference in direction, according as the "Back scratch" (crossing the foot over in front), the I B cross-roll, or the ordinary stroke of I B edge is employed, has been pointed out in the treatise on "Striking" (Chapter III.),[54] and it is necessary to agree on the stroke to be adopted, as unless uniformity in this respect is observed the skaters will take the fresh stroke at different angles, and throw the figure out of the square.

Form to be observed in skating "twice back"

Care should be taken in "twice back" to make each turn a *bonâ fide* three, skated in the correct form, and not to rush at the turn without preparation, whip round, and drop on to the O B edge immediately, as is too

---

[54] Pages 54–57.

commonly the case. The latter results in a scrambling performance, and the O B edge is invariably taken up too far from the other foot, entailing loss of power and steadiness. The O B edge should in this movement be practically a continuation of the curve of I B edge previously skated by the other foot, thus,

the common error being to skate it in the following manner:

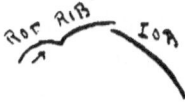

The same principle applies in all cases where the trend of the fresh curve follows the same direction as the previous edge, unless for special reasons the direction of the new curve is intentionally made to deviate from that of the preceding one.

Apart from such considerations of form, the manner in which any movement should be skated, it must be understood, is purely a matter of individual opinion, and not a question of good or bad skating. Recognised methods are merely expedient for the sake of uniformity.

Care should be taken to strike off on a light edge

Care should also be taken to strike off on a light edge when taking a fresh stroke, since it is perfectly easy to get harder on the edge if necessary, but difficult to get more lightly on it to rectify matters if any rotation has been set up, which is a likely contingency in the case of beginners, unless they avoid a hard edge in the first instance. But the principle of skating on a light edge must not lead to spurious turns approached absolutely on the flat of the blade with a corresponding straight line after.

The centre should not be too anxiously watched the whole time

A beginner, too, is apt to be over anxious to keep his eye on the centre the whole time, which often prevents his travelling in the correct attitude for the edge he is on. During a figure there are sure to be moments when it is impossible to look either at the centre or one's partner without prejudice to one's own skating. Unless the skating be very erratic, the skater will find the centre, so to speak, come to him at the right moment, and he must at times give his partner credit for doing his duty without anxiously watching his movements, though whenever practicable he should keep his eye on both.

Imaginary lines and their use

The proportions assigned by usage to various movements will be seen by studying the elementary figures given further on. Every skater should have a general idea of the approximate shape and proportion usually given to the various calls, and when practising them *alone* should endeavour to skate them so that the different curves of which the figure is composed are confined to the quarter of the circle assigned to them by custom.

The whole figure, it must be borne in mind, is constantly shifting round; hence, supposing the original imaginary lines, down which the four skaters start in the first instance, to point due north, south, east, and west, it does not follow that, on returning to the centre, the imaginary lines for the next movement will exactly coincide with the previous ones. The question of lines, however, should only occupy the skater's mind when practising *alone*, and to some extent if he be leading a combined set. This is the legitimate use of these imaginary lines, whereas some over-conscientious skaters allow them to absorb their attention to the detriment of the figure as a combined movement.

The caller alone is responsible for manner of skating figure

Once embarked in a combined set, all thought of lines must be completely dismissed from the mind, except in the case of the caller, whose duty it is to set the style of skating the movement. *He* would do well to skate the figure in the orthodox manner, that is, in the manner generally recognised by usage, lest the other skaters should fail to imitate his eccentricities; but, as regards, the other performers, their duty is solely to watch, and imitate, the caller.

Imitation sole duty of other skaters

So long as the figure be satisfactorily skated as a combined movement, it matters little whether the component parts of it fall exactly within the prescribed limits. Whether they do so, or not, is a question which rests entirely with the caller, imitation being the sole duty of the others. Only the caller has any discretionary judgment, and all individual opinion as to the exact manner in which the figure should be proportioned must give way to the imperative necessity of keeping square. Once the haunting idea of lines and quarters of circles is allowed to influence the actions of any but the caller, the figure at once ceases to be a series of combined movements, and the set is entirely spoilt.

In studying the figures which follow, the beginner should bear in mind, then, the object and legitimate use of the division of the circle into segments by imaginary lines.

How to practise elementary figures

The elementary figures, in which none but simple turns occur, are not arranged in sets, since constant repetition of each, on either foot, is rather desirable, as practice, than skating through a certain number without a pause. Those that do not naturally alternate can be made to do so by introducing a forward entire, or inside forward entire, at the end of the call. The diagrams, in every case, represent the calls as skated commencing with the right foot.

Calls requiring a centre Mohawk or Choctaw without notification

As a rule, when a back edge is taken up at the centre after a forward edge, it is merely the second half of a Mohawk, or Choctaw, which has been named in the call, and the next movement is then commenced on the other foot.

In rare cases, however, the back edge of the Mohawk, or Choctaw, is made to serve as the first curve of the succeeding movement, in which case the word "Mohawk," or "Choctaw," does not necessarily occur in the call. For instance, "*Once back,* AND *forward meet,* AND *once forward meet,*" is a figure of this description, and it is only possible by combining the forward edge approaching, and the back edge leaving, the centre, in the form of a centre Mohawk. Thus:

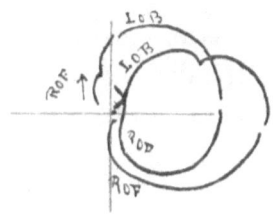

The clearest method of calling this figure is "*Once back,* AND *forward centre Mohawk, turn,* AND *forward,*" but if called in the former manner, the skaters should realise at once that a centre Mohawk must be skated, unless a cross-Mohawk be preferred, though the word "Mohawk" does not occur.

Of all catch calls perhaps the most likely to create confusion and spoil the set is the following:

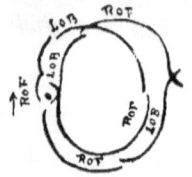

Once back, AND *forward*, AND *back two Mohawks meet*.

The proper way to call it is this—

Once back, AND *forward centre Mohawk*, AND *forward Mohawk*, AND *forward*.

Of course the back edge of the first Mohawk and the forward edge of the second Mohawk can be regarded as a back Mohawk, as also the back edge of the second Mohawk and the subsequent forward edge; but a Mohawk is necessary in both cases to take up the back edge, and the call "back two Mohawks" is really inexcusable except as a joke.

The above explanations are necessary to prevent the beginner from being taken by surprise by catch calls, which are sometimes made use of by facetious callers to trap the unwary.

Alternative method of skating outside Choctaw in order to gain impetus

In figures of this class, in the case of the outside Choctaw it is difficult to obtain any fresh impetus, where such is needed, owing to the fact that the inclination required for the fresh curve converges towards the previous inclination of the body, precluding the possibility of a vigorous shove from the foot as it leaves the ice, since this would have the effect of forcing the skate over on to the outside edge, resulting in a Mohawk. The following diagrams will make this easily intelligible.

OUTSIDE CHOCTAW.

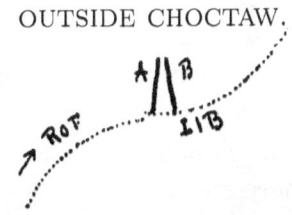

A. Inclination of body on O F edge.
B. Inclination of body on I B edge.

In the case of B turns skated on alternate feet to a centre, for example, the movement becomes more and more laboured, from the inability to gain sufficient impetus by means of the ordinary Choctaw. Some expedient therefore has to be adopted to remedy this.

The cross-Choctaw is one alternative, but for most people is only possible by means of a jump. The following method therefore of getting on to the I B edge after the O F edge, in this particular movement, is suggested—namely, that, when in the attitude required for a Choctaw, the unemployed leg should be swung in front of the other, with the toe well turned out, and the foot be dropped on the ice, so that the feet are toe to toe. Thus:

The other foot leaves the ice in the act of making an O F counter, the instant the foot about to take up the I B edge touches it, and a vigorous shove from the toe of the skate, at this moment, gives the necessary impetus for the succeeding movement. This method has the further advantage that the unemployed leg is from the first carried behind in the right position for the B turn, which is not the case when the ordinary Choctaw is skated. This stroke is somewhat difficult, but, luckily, the necessity for its use is exceedingly rare.

In the case of a certain number of the following figures, such suggestions are made as are likely to be of use, the rest calling for no special remarks.

Elementary calls

Explanation respecting diagrams

The *black* lines are the *right* foot, the *red*[55] lines the *left* foot. An arrow at the beginning of a curve, thus: indicates that the movement is *back wards*. Where there is no arrow head, the movement is forwards. This system renders explanatory letters unnecessary.

N.B.—Those figures which do not naturally alternate, are indicated by an asterisk, thus *.

---

[55]Gray in the paperack edition.

1. Forward entire.

2. Inside forward entire.

3. Forward three entire.

4. Inside forward three entire.

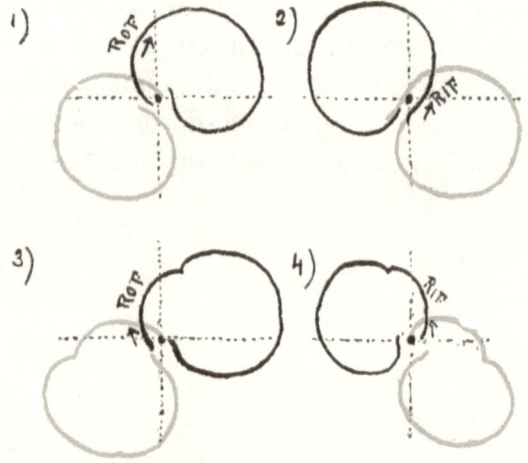

DIAGRAM 2.—The stroke should be taken just before the centre is reached, for fear of disturbing it in the act of striking.

DIAGRAM 3.—In threes to a centre—the tail should occupy two-thirds of the circle. Before taking up the O F edge at the centre, after the previous three, the body must prepare as if for an I B counter.

DIAGRAM 4.—In threes to a centre—the tail should occupy two-thirds of the circle. Before taking up the I F edge at the centre, after the previous three, the body must prepare as if for an O B rocker.

5. Forward, *and* forward three, *and* forward.

6. Forward, *and* I F three, *and* forward.

7. Forward, *and* I F off pass, *and* forward.

8. I F, *and* forward off pass, *and* I F entire.

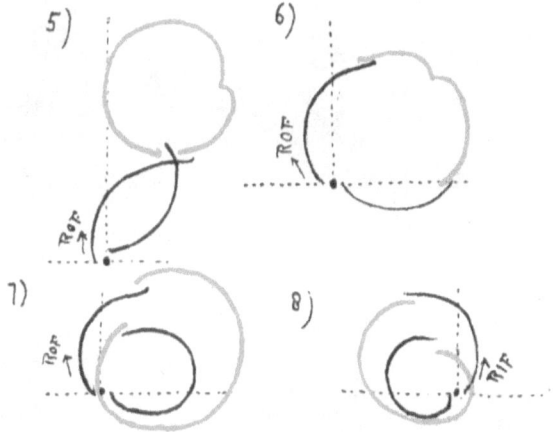

DIAGRAM 6.—The skater should not look towards the centre on taking up the I F edge, but over the shoulder of the employed leg. Before taking up the O F edge after the tree, body must prepare as if for a D turn.

DIAGRAM 7.—The skater should not at once look towards the centre on taking up I F edge.

DIAGRAM 8.—The skater should not be in too great a hurry to look for the centre on O F edge.

9. Twice back, *and* forward.

10. Twice back, *and* forward three.

11. Twice back, *and* forward off pass entire.

*12. Once back, *and* forward, *and* I F pass entire off.

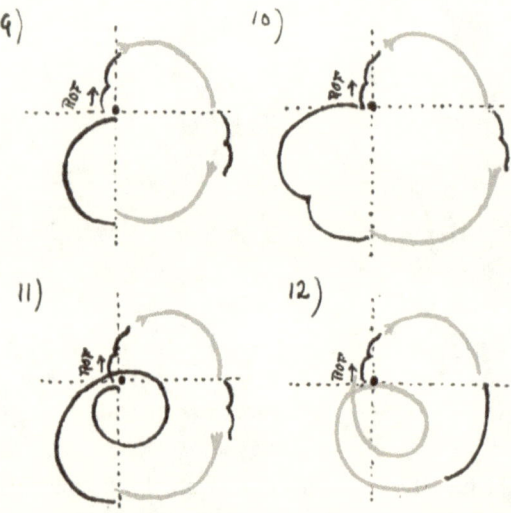

DIAGRAM 9.—Before taking up the O F edge, after the O B edge on the other foot, the body must prepare as if for a D turn.

DIAGRAM 12.—Alternates with "forward entire."

English Skating

13. Forward two turns entire.

14. Inside forward two turns entire.

15. Forward three turns entire.

16. Inside forward three turns entire.

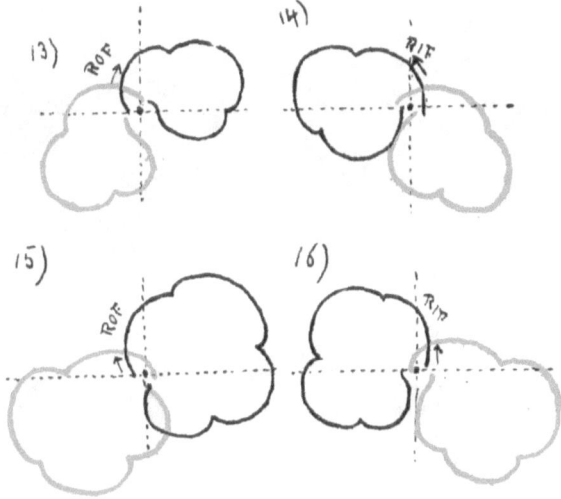

DIAGRAMS 13 AND 14.—In two turns entire, on either edge, the second turn should be postponed till the centre is visible while preparing for the turn in the orthodox manner.

DIAGRAMS 15 AND 16.—In three turns entire, on either edge, the second turn should be made the moment it is *possible* to catch sight of the centre over the shoulder. (*See* remarks on preparation, Nos. 3 and 4.)

180   English Skating

17. Forward, *and* forward two turns, *and* forward.

18. I F, *and* I F two turns, *and* I F.

19. Twice back, *and* forward centre change entire off.

*20. Once back, *and* forward, *and* forward inside centre change entire.

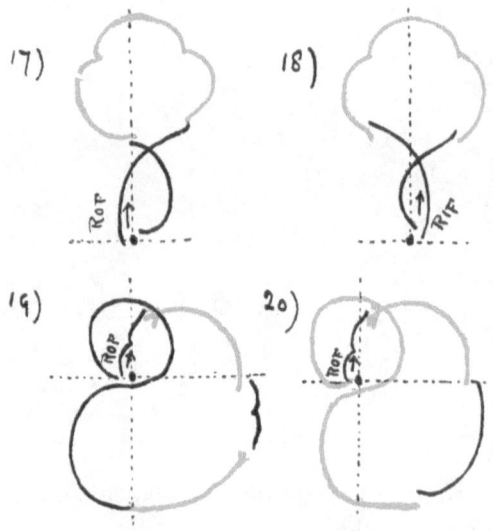

DIAGRAM 20.—Alternates with "forward entire."

English Skating 181

*21. Twice back, centre change entire.

22. Once back, *and* inside back, centre change entire, off.

*23. Twice back meet, *and* back, *and* forward three.

24. Twice back off meet, *and* forward three entire.

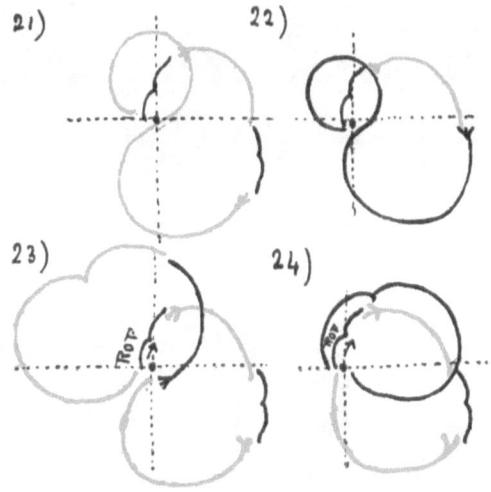

DIAGRAM 21.—Alternates with "forward entire."
DIAGRAM 22.—The change of edge is facilitated by looking back over employed shoulder.
DIAGRAM 23.—Alternates with "forward entire." Back edge at centre to be taken up with cross roll.

182 English Skating

*25. Once back, *and* forward three about, *and* once back, *and* forward.

26. Once back about, *and* I F three off.

27. Twice back, *and* forward off centre turn entire.

*28. Once back, *and* forward, *and* I F off centre turn entire, off.

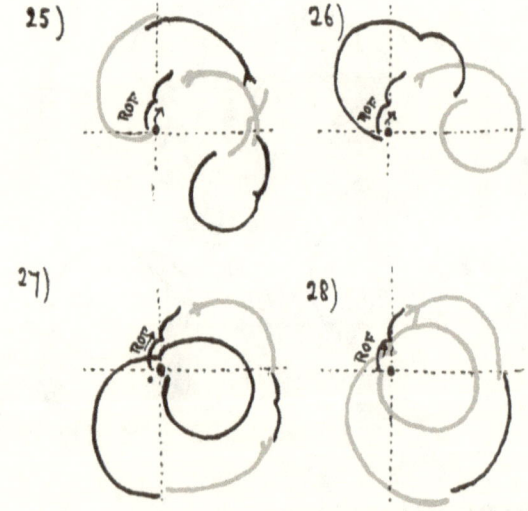

Diagrams 25 and 28.—Alternate with "forward entire."

*29. Twice back, turn, meet.

30. Once, back, and I B, turn, meet.

*31. Twice back, off centre turn entire off.

32. Once back, and I B off centre turn entire.

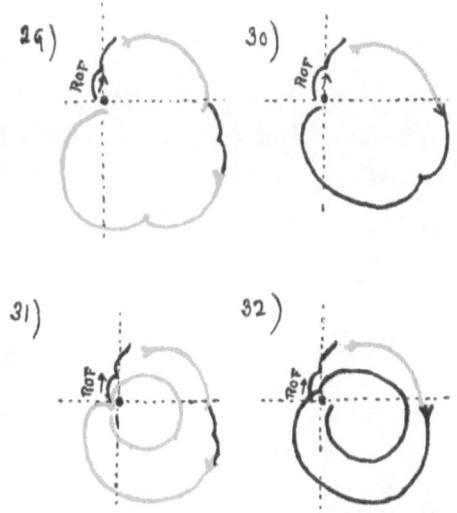

DIAGRAM 29.—Alternates with "inside forward entire off."
DIAGRAM 31.—Alternates with "forward entire." Look well over shoulder o employed leg, that is, away from the centre, after the off centre turn, and get very lightly on the I F edge, to avoid curling in.
DIAGRAM 32.—The I B may be taken up with a step of the "back scratch" if the skater desires to cut straight for the centre, rather than continue circling round the circumference.

184 English Skating

29. Twice back, *and* forward Q off meet.

*30. Once back, *and* forward, *and* I F Q.

*31. Twice back, back Q.

32. Once back, *and* I B Q off meet.

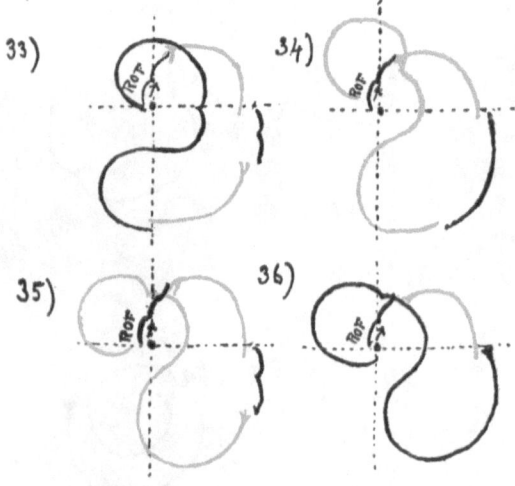

DIAGRAM 34.—Alternates with "forward entire."
DIAGRAM 35.—Alternates with "forward entire." The B turn should not be hurried, but full value should be given to the I B edge after the change.

English Skating 185

37. Twice back, *and* forward centre change Q entire, off.

*38. Once back, *and* forward, *and* I F centre change Q entire.

*39. Twice back, back centre change Q entire.

40. Once back, *and* I B centre change Q entire, off.

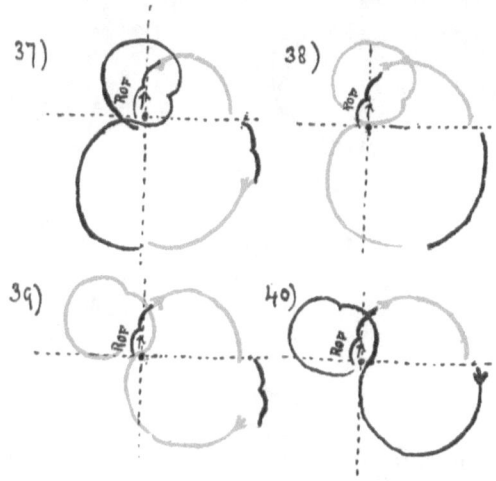

DIAGRAM 38.—Alternates with "forward entire."
DIAGRAM 39.—Alternates with "forward entire." The B turn should not be hurried, but full value should be given to the I B edge after the change.

41. Forward, *and* I F Q about, *and* forward.

42. I F, *and* forward Q about, *and* I F.

43. Inside twice back, *and* I F three.

*44. Once back about, *and* inside once back off meet.

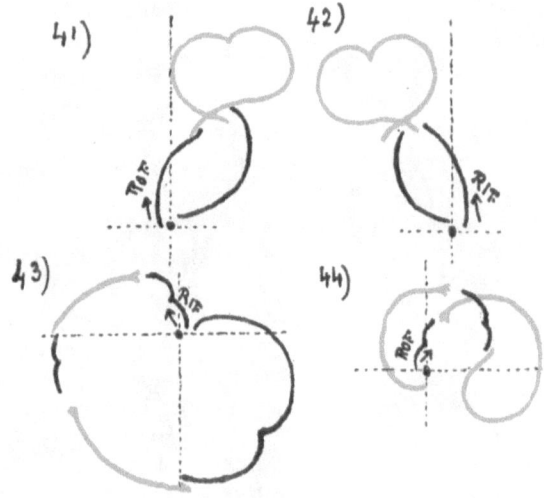

DIAGRAM 43.—The I B edge should be taken up by placing the foot behind the other, very slightly crossed, toe to heel. The stroke is taken with a straight leg, the thrust being from the toe of the skate.

DIAGRAM 44.—Alternates with "inside forward entire off."

English Skating 187

*45. Inside once back about, *and* once back off meet.

*46. Inside once back meet, *and* I B, *and* I F three.

*47. Forward Q out, *and* forward reverse Q in.

*48. Inside forward Q out, *and* inside forward reverse Q in.

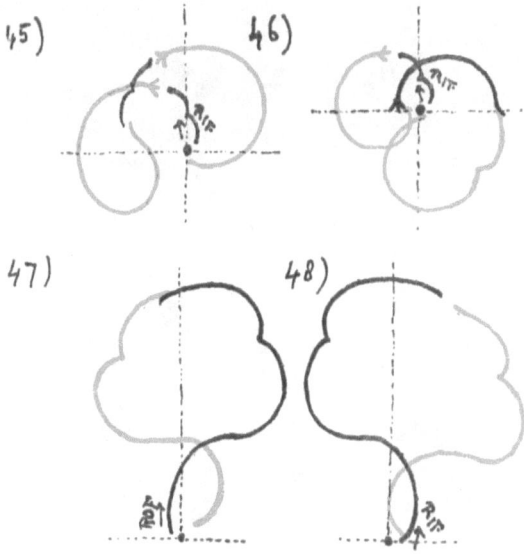

DIAGRAMS 45 AND 48.—Alternate with "forward entire off."
DIAGRAM 46.—Alternates with "inside forward entire."
DIAGRAM 47.—Alternates with "inside forward entire off."

188 English Skating

49. Twice back, *and* forward reverse Q, off meet.

*50. Once back, *and* forward, *and* I F reverse Q, off meet.

*51. Twice back, reverse Q meet.

52. Once back, *and* I B reverse Q, off meet.

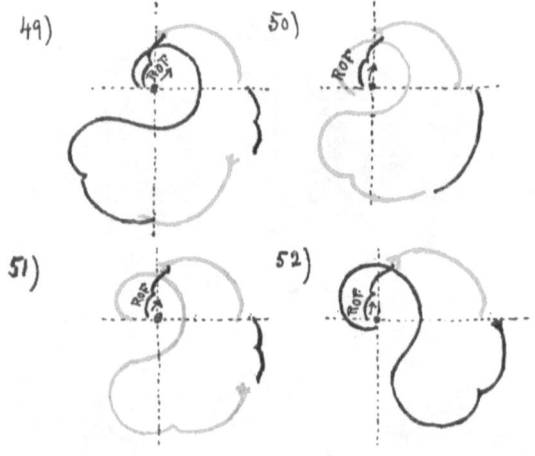

DIAGRAM 50.—Alternates with "inside forward entire off."
DIAGRAM 51.—Alternates with "forward entire."

---

*53. Twice back, *and* forward three, *and* I F three.

*54. Twice back, *and* forward three turns, *and* back meet, *and* back two turns, *and* forward

*55. Once back, *and* forward three about, *and* forward off centre Mohawk, *and* forward.

*56. Once back, *and* forward about, turn, *and* inside once back, *and* inside off centre Mohawk, *and* I F.

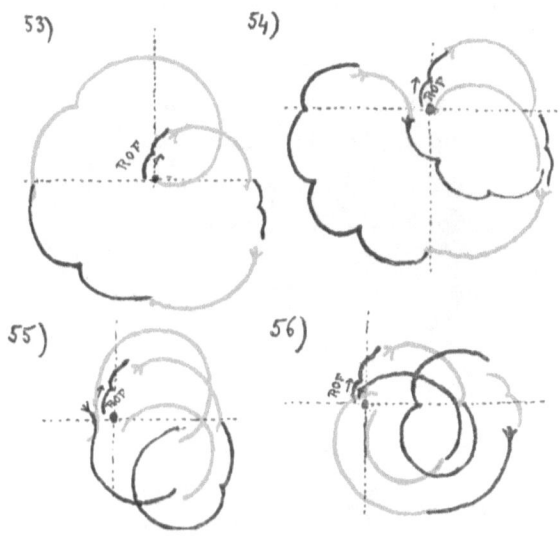

DIAGRAM 54.—Alternates with "forward entire." After the third turn, the skater should make straight for the centre on the I B edge, and not continue round the circumference. On taking O B cross-roll at centre, he should get very lightly on edge to avoid too much rotation.

DIAGRAM 53.—Alternates with "inside forward entire off." On tail of forward three, look well over unemployed shoulder, away from the centre, since a very sideways attitude on I B edge is necessary in order to take up the I F edge satisfactorily. The body must prepare as if for an I B bracket.

DIAGRAM 55.—Alternates with "forward entire."

DIAGRAM 56.—Alternates with "inside forward entire off."

190 English Skating

*57. Once back meet, *and* back entire, *and* back entire.

58. Once back, *and* I B meet, *and* I B entire, *and* I B entire.

59. Once back about, turn, *and* once back pass entire *and* back entire off.

60. Inside once back about, turn, *and* inside once back pass entire, *and* inside back entire off.

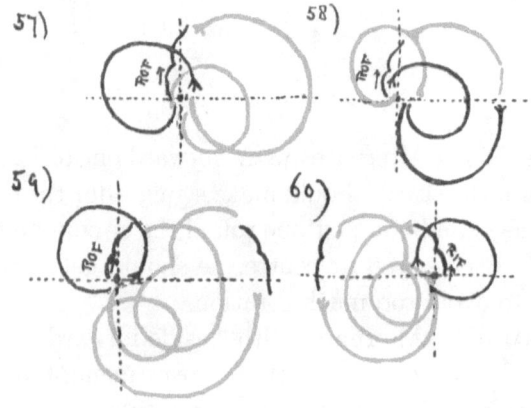

DIAGRAM 57.—Alternates with "inside forward entire off."

DIAGRAM 59.—After passing the centre on the O B in order to skate the complete circle and keep on a right edge, the skater should look back at the centre till half the circle is completed. The effect is that a larger circle is skated, while at the same time preventing the cramped feeling produced by twisting round in a smaller space.

DIAGRAM 60.—Care must be taken not to attempt the B turn till the unemployed leg is well behind and a sideways attitude has been adopted—then the turn must be prepared for deliberately in the proper manner. The centre should be passed before taking up the I B entire, to avoid the risk of disturbing it during the stroke, or when bringing the leg behind immediately after.

Dismiss calls

1. Once back, change out, dismiss.

2. Forward Mohawk, change out, dismiss.

3. Forward Q, change out, dismiss.

4. Forward, *and* I F about Mohawk, dismiss.

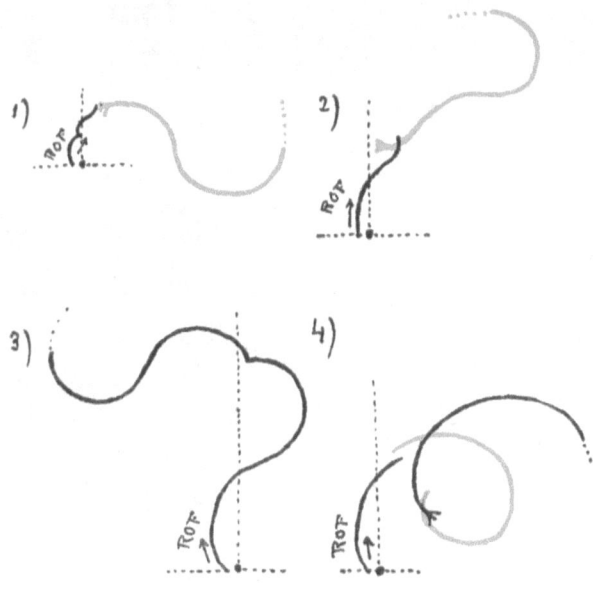

Difficult calls for advanced skaters

The following sets of calls are for advanced skaters alone. The published sets of calls are for the most part advisedly more or less elementary, or they would be of little general use. First-class skaters, however, require something more to put them on their mettle, and, as their number is happily increasing year by year, calls requiring a higher standard of proficiency should eventually be in more frequent demand. The following sets, all of which have been proved feasible in practice, will, it is hoped, to a certain extent, meet these requirements, and suggest new and more difficult combinations for the enjoyment of experts.

Some of the calls included in these sets have been contributed by Mr. E. Collingwood, of the Davos Skating Club.

Diagrams are in some cases given, showing the placing of the figures.[56]

---

[56]The unnumbered diagram at the end (when present) is the dismiss call, i.e., the italicized call at the end of the set.

Set I

Nos. 1–6 may be repeated with Counters instead of Rockers.

1. Once back *and* forward about rocker off meet } repeat.

2. Once back *and* forward, *and* I F about rocker meet

3. Forward Choctaw, bracket, about, *and* forward

} repeat.

4. Twice back, about, rocker meet
5. Forward Mohawk, bracket, *and* forward

} repeat.

6. Once back, *and* I B about, rocker off meet } repeat.

7. Inside once back, *and* I F off, *and* inside once forward

8. Inside once reverse back, *and* once reverse back, *and* I F turn about, *and* I F off centre Mohawk entire

9. Once back, *and* forward meet, *and* twice forward

10. Once reverse back, *and* inside once reverse back, *and* O F turn about, *and* O F centre Choctaw, turn, *and* I F

} repeat.

Once back, and *forward about, Mohawk, change, dismiss.*

English Skating 197

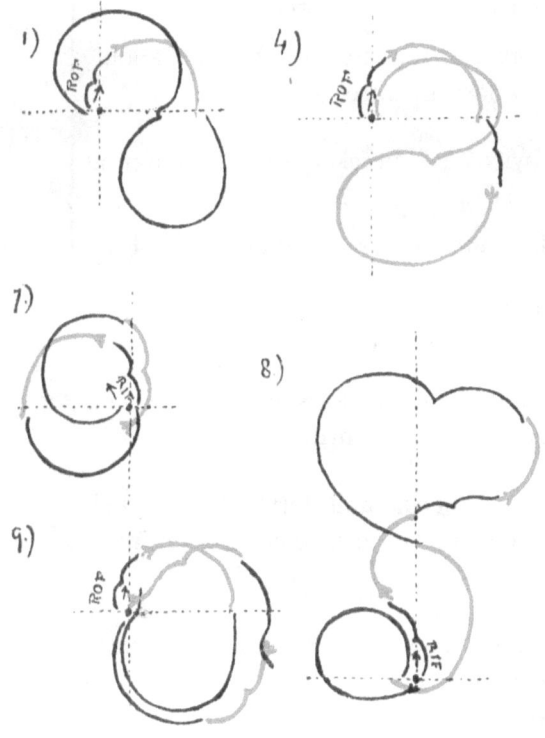

Set II

1. Twice back, *and* forward bracket about, counter off meet } repeat.

2. Twice back, *and* forward, *and* I F bracket about, counter meet
3. Forward, *and* forward bracket about, *and* forward meet } repeat.

4. Twice back, bracket, about, counter off meet
5. I F, *and* I F bracket about, *and* I F off } repeat.

6. Twice back, *and* I B bracket about, counter off meet } repeat.

7. Twice back, *and* forward about, rocker, centre counter entire } repeat.

8. Twice back, *and* forward, *and* I F about, rocker, centre counter entire
9. I F bracket entire off } repeat.

10. Twice back about, rocker, centre counter entire off
11. Forward bracket entire } repeat.

12. Twice back, *and* I B about, rocker, centre counter entire } repeat.

Once back, and *forward,* and *I F about, bracket, change dismiss.*

English Skating

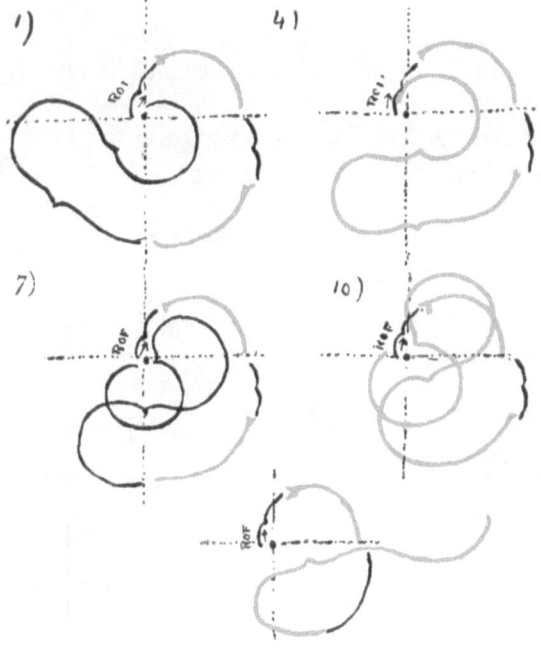

Set III

1. Once back, *and* forward about, bracket, *and* I F about, Choctaw off meet } repeat.

2. Once back, *and* forward, *and* I F about, bracket, *and* O F about, Choctaw off meet
3. I F Mohawk, *and* I F turn off meet } repeat.

4. Twice back, about, bracket, *and* forward about, counter off meet } repeat.

5. Once back, *and* I B about, bracket, *and* I F about, counter meet
6. Forward, *and* I F off centre Mohawk entire } repeat.

7. Once back, *and* forward about, counter, bracket, off meet } repeat.

8. Once back, *and* forward, *and* I F about, counter, bracket, meet
9. Forward Mohawk, *and* I B off centre rocker entire off } repeat.

10. Once back, *and* I B about, counter, bracket, off meet } repeat.

Forward, and *inside once back, rocker, Mohawk, dismiss.*

English Skating 201

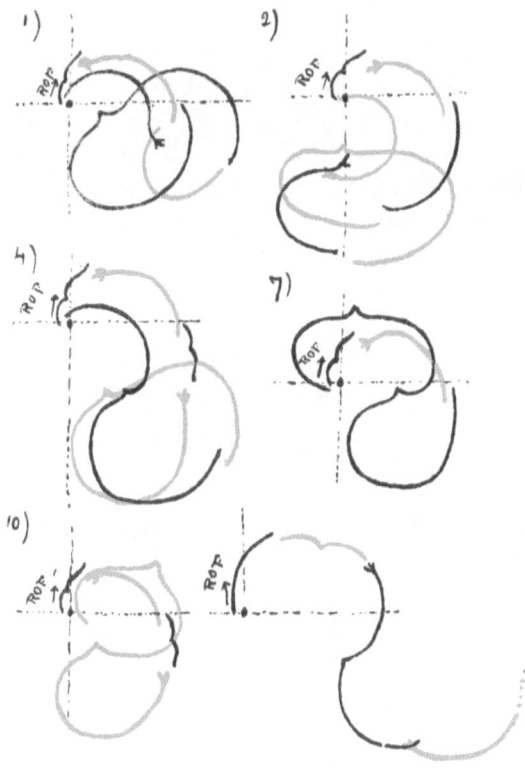

Set IV

1. Once back, *and* forward, about, bracket, *and* I F about, bracket, about, counter off meet
2. I F, *and* forward centre Mohawk, *and* I B off centre rocker entire off
3. Forward Choctaw about, rocker off pass, *and* O F bracket entire

} repeat.

4. Once back, *and* forward, *and* I F about, bracket, *and* outside forward about, bracket, about, counter off meet

} repeat.

5. Twice back about, bracket, I F Mohawk about, bracket, O F Mohawk about, counter meet
6. O F *and* I F off centre Mohawk, *and* O B off centre rocker entire off
7. I F Choctaw about, rocker off pass, *and* I F bracket entire off

} repeat.

8. Once back, *and* I B about, bracket, O F Mohawk about, bracket, I F Mohawk about, counter off meet

} repeat.

9. O F bracket, turn, bracket, entire off
10. I F bracket, turn, bracket, entire
11. I F turn, bracket, turn, entire off
12. O F turn, racket, turn, entire
13. O F Mohawk, *and* OF

} repeat.

English Skating

Forward Choctaw, about, turn, Choctaw, dismiss

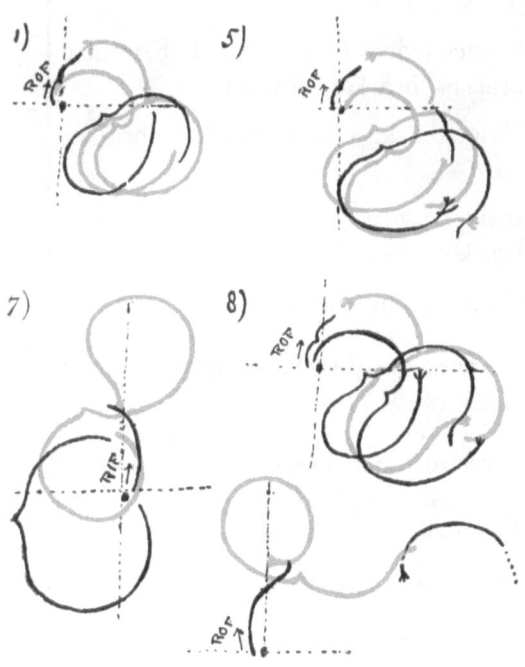

Set V

1. Twice back, off centre turn, bracket entire off
2. Bracket, turn, bracket, entire

} repeat.

3. Twice back *and* forward centre bracket, bracket off meet
4. Inside twice back, *and* I F centre bracket, bracket off meet
5. Twice back, centre bracket, bracket meet
6. Inside twice back, centre bracket, bracket meet
7. Counter, out about, counter meet

} repeat.

8. Forward two brackets, centre counter entire off } repeat.

9. Forward three, bracket entire } repeat.

10. Mohawk, centre bracket entire
11. Inside two brackets entire off

} repeat.

12. Bracket about, counter off meet } repeat.

13. Forward, *and* I F turn, bracket meet
14. I F turn, centre bracket entire off

} repeat.

Forward, and *I F turn about, change, bracket, Choctaw, dismiss*

English Skating 205

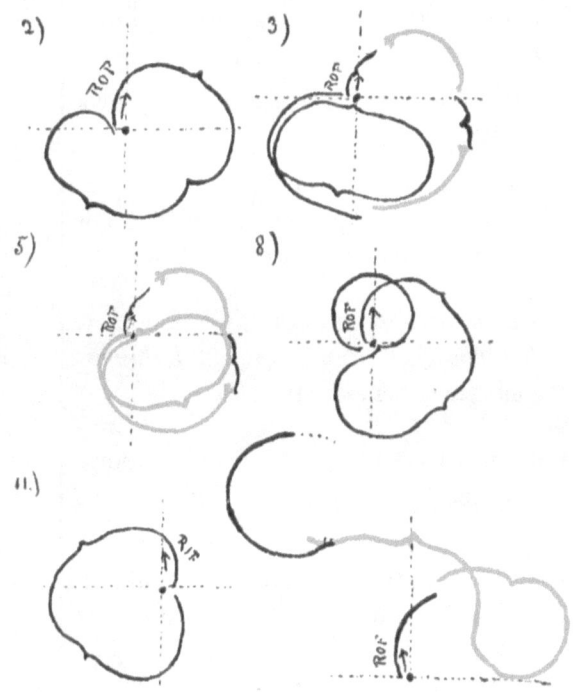

Set VI

1. Twice back, counter out, *and* I F about Choctaw meet
2. Inside twice back, counter out, *and* O F about Choctaw meet
3. Forward Choctaw about, *and* forward

} repeat.

4. Forward three, I B bracket, Mohawk meet

5. I F three, O B bracket, inside Mohawk meet

6. Forward two brackets, *and* I F Choctaw out, bracket about, *and* I F about, Choctaw off meet

} repeat.

7. I F two brackets, *and* O F Choctaw out, bracket about, *and* O F about, Choctaw off meet (repeat).

} repeat.

8. Forward counter out, change, about, counter, about, *and* I F Mohawk, *and* I F meet

9. I F counter out, change, about, counter, about, *and* O F Mohawk, *and* O F meet

10. Forward Choctaw about, *and* forward

} repeat.

11. Twice back meet, *and* twice forward meet

12. Once reverse back about, *and* I B meet, *and* twice inside reverse forward, *and* I F about, change about, Choctaw meet

} repeat.

Forward counter out, and *forward Choctaw, dismiss.*

English Skating

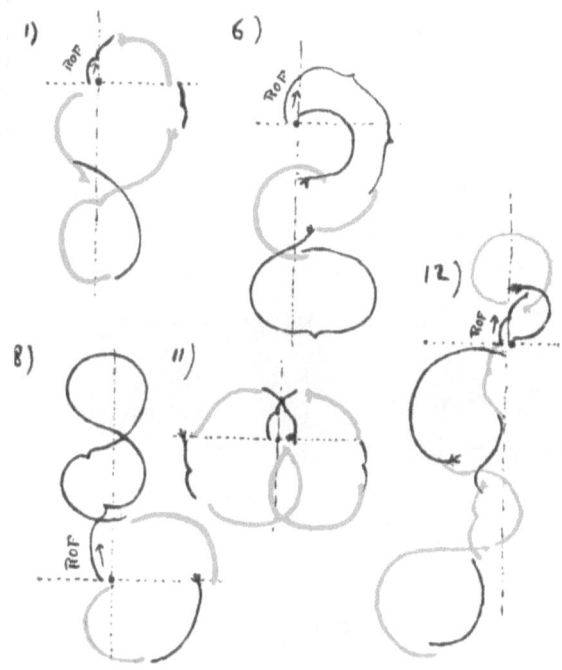

N.B.—Nos. 11 and 12 are given as above, since this form of calling is sometimes made use of. The clearer and better way of calling is as follows:—

11. Twice back meet, *and* O B turn, *and* forward Mohawk, turn, *and* O F

12. Forward 3, *and* I B about, *and* I B meet, *and* I B turn, *and* forward Choctaw, turn, *and* O F, *and* I F about, change about Choctaw meet

} repeat.

Set VII

1. Once back, *and* O F about, counter centre bracket entire, off } repeat.

2. Once back, *and* O F, *and* I F about, counter, centre bracket entire off
3. I F Mohawk, centre rocker, Mohawk meet
} repeat.

4. Twice back about, counter, centre bracket entire
5. Forward Mohawk, off centre rocker Mohawk off meet
} repeat.

6. Once back, *and* I B about, counter, centre bracket entire off } repeat.

7. Once back, *and* forward bracket, about, *and* I B off centre turn entire off
8. Inside once back, *and* I F bracket about, *and* O B off centre turn entire off
9. Inside once back, *and* I F bracket about, *and* O B off centre turn entire off
10. Twice back, bracket about, *and* I F off centre turn entire off
11. Once back, *and* I B bracket about, *and* forward off centre turn entire
} repeat.

English Skating

12. Forward Choctaw, turn, *and* I F about, *and* I F off centre Mohawk turn entire } repeat.

13. Forward Mohawk entire
14. I F Choctaw, turn, *and* forward about, *and* forward off centre Mohawk turn entire off } repeat.

Forward rocker, bracket, turn, change, dismiss.

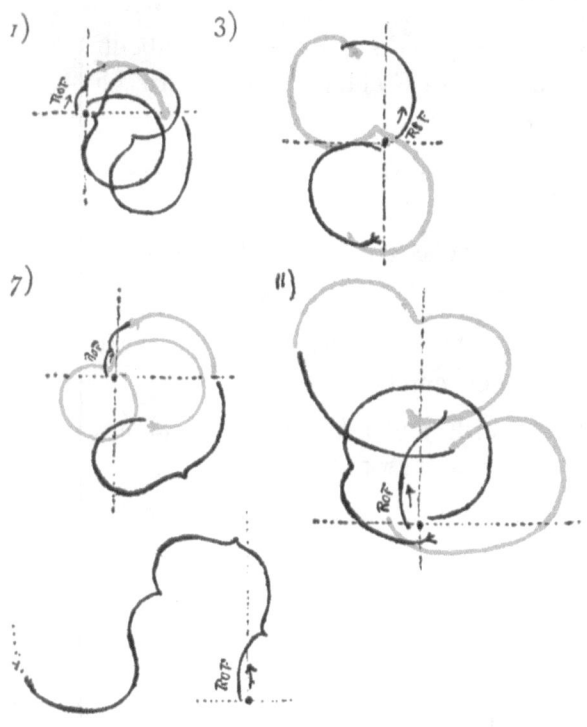

Set VIII

1. Forward, *and* I F counter out about, counter about, Choctaw meet
2. I F rocker, bracket, *and* I F off meet
3. Bracket entire, *and* I B turn about, counter off meet
4. Forward Choctaw about, counter, centre change, *and* I F two brackets, *and* O F meet

} repeat.

5. Forward, *and* I F counter out about, turn, *and* I F about counter, turn, off meet
6. I F Choctaw, bracket, *and* forward bracket meet
7. Bracket once back, *and* I B centre turn, bracket meet

} repeat.

8. Twice back about, counter, centre counter, *and* O F meet
9. Forward, *and* I F rocker out about, rocker, Mohawk off meet
10. I F rocker out, *and* back about, rocker meet
11. Forward entire, centre Mohawk, turn, centre Choctaw, turn, entire off
12. Forward entire, centre Choctaw, turn, centre Choctaw, turn, entire
13. Bracket entire

} repeat.

English Skating 211

Forward turn, and *forward bracket, turn, Choctaw, dismiss.*

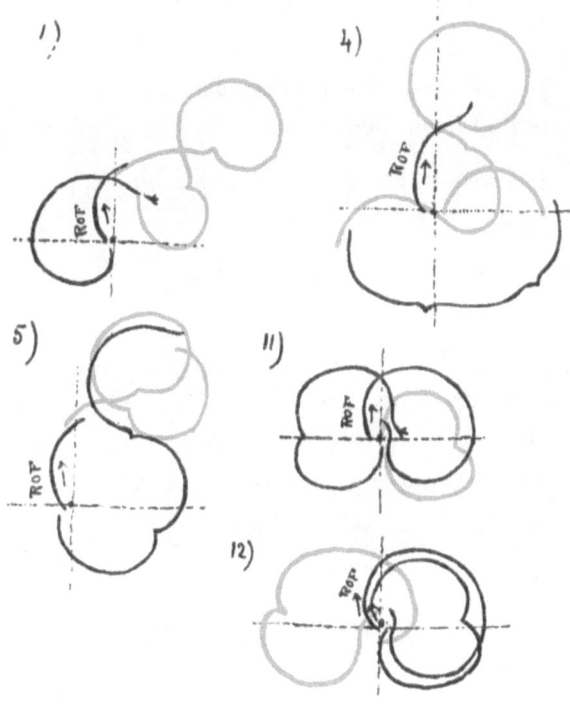

Set IX

1. I F two counters, *and* I B about, change about, rocker off meet
2. I F Mohawk, centre turn, bracket entire
3. Forward Choctaw about, *and* I B about rocker meet

} repeat.

4. Inside twice back, centre turn, counter, *and* O F off meet } repeat.

5. I F rocker out about, *and* O F about, counter off meet
6. Forward, *and* I F Choctaw about, change about, *and* O F meet

} repeat.

7. I F, *and* I F rocker, *and* back about, change about, *and* I B centre rocker entire
8. I F Choctaw out, bracket entire off
9. Forward bracket, *and* I B turn, bracket about, *and* O F off meet

} repeat.

10. Twice inside back, turn, off centre Choctaw, turn entire
11. Twice back, turn, off centre Choctaw, turn, off centre Mohawk entire off

} repeat.

I F counter, and *back about, bracket, rocker, dismiss.*

English Skating

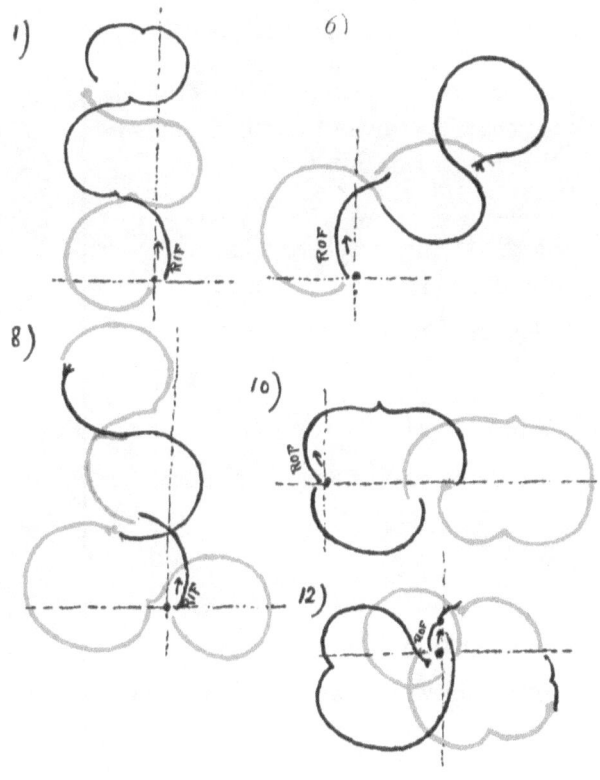

Set X

1. I F bracket, *and* I B centre counter, Mohawk meet
2. Forward rocker about, counter, Choctaw, *and* I B bracket meet, *and* forward bracket, turn entire off

} repeat.

3. Twice back, rocker, Mohawk about, rocker, Choctaw out about about, *and* O F bracket off meet
4. Twice inside back, rocker, inside Mohawk about, rocker, Choctaw out about about, *and* I F bracket meet
5. I F turn, bracket, entire off

} repeat.

6. O F rocker out, about, *and* I F about, counter meet
7. O F Mohawk out, *and* I B about, *and* I B centre rocker Mohawk, bracket meet

} repeat.

8. Once reverse back, *and* inside once back, turn, bracket, off meet
9. Inside forward, turn, bracket about, Mohawk, rocker meet
10. Inside Mohawk, bracket, Mohawk off meet

} repeat.

Forward counter, and *I B about, rocker, change, turn, dismiss.*

English Skating 215

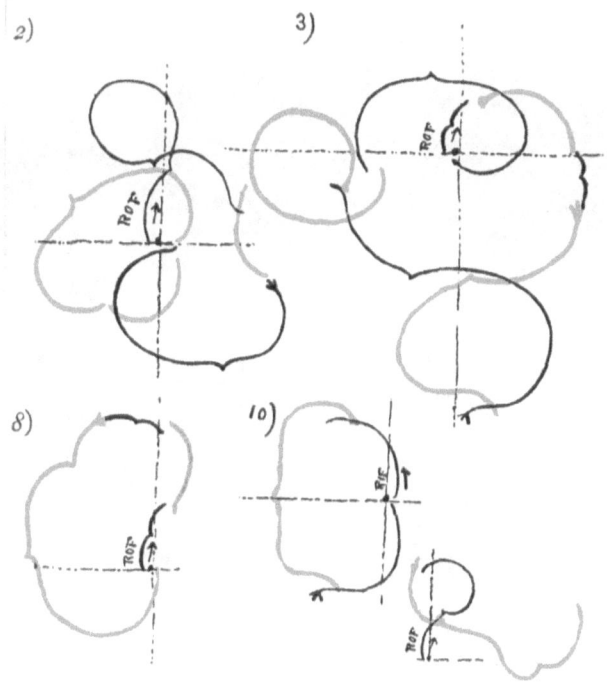

Appendix I. Hand-in-hand skating

All movements used in combined figure-skating can be skated side by side, the skaters holding one, or both, hands. Such movements are known as "scuds." As, for the most part, one of the skaters has to follow in the other's tracks, it is necessary for both to know, without hesitation, when to precede, and when to let the other skater run ahead.

Rules of precedence in side-by-side scuds

The following simple rules, if borne in mind, will prevent all doubt on the subject; they are equally applicable whether the movement begins backwards or forwards.

Simple turn rocker; serpentine followed by counter, or bracket

First curve on *outside edge*, skater on *inside foot* precedes.
First curve on *inside edge*, skater on *outside foot* precedes.

Bracket; counter; serpentine followed by simple turn, or rocker

First curve on *outside edge*, skater on *outside foot* precedes.
First curve on *inside edge*, skater on *inside foot* precedes.

Mohawks; Choctaws

Skater on *outside foot* precedes.

[N.B.—"Precedes" means runs ahead in the direction of progress, whether forwards or backwards. The right foot of the right-hand, and the left foot of the left-hand skater, are of course the outside feet.]

Possible use of side-by-side scuds in combined figure-skating

All calls used in combined figure-skating are capable of being skated as scuds. Hence it is possible for eight people, skating in pairs, hand-in-hand, to take part in a combined figure to a centre, instead of four only, skating in the usual way.

It is not within the scope of this little book to deal exhaustively with this branch of the art, which has been fully treated of in other works on skating. It is merely touched on owing to the possible use, in the future, of the hand-in-hand style in combined figure-skating.

A selected *répertoire*, however, for practice, of side-by-side scuds and of face-to-face scuds recommended by experience, is here annexed.

Side-by-side scuds

Selected répertoire of side-by-side scuds

1. Forward Q, *and* forward, *and* forward.

2. Forward inside Q, *and* forward, *and* forward.

3. Forward reverse Q, *and* back, *and* forward.

4. Inside forward reverse Q, *and* back, *and* forward.

5. Mohawk, *and* I B, *and* I F, *and* forward. ["Circular Mohawk" with addition of O F, to make it alternate.]

English Skating

6. Once back, *and* I F Mohawk, back change, *and* back.

7. Rocker (pass), *and* forward, *and* forward.

8. $\left\{\begin{array}{l}\text{Rocker}\\ \text{Counter}\end{array}\right\}$ pass, *and* back, *and* forward. [On right food, right-hand skater does counter, and *vice-versâ*.

9. Two turns, *and* forward, *and* forward.

10. Back two turns, *and* back, *and* back.

11. Forward, *and* $\left\{\begin{array}{l}\text{I F rocker}\\ \text{I F counter}\end{array}\right\}$ *and* I F. [Skater on the outside foot does the rocker.]

12. $\left\{\begin{array}{l}\text{Forward three}\\ \text{Bracket}\end{array}\right\}$ *and* back, *and* $\left\{\begin{array}{l}\text{forward three}\\ \text{bracket}\end{array}\right\}$ *and* back, *and* back. [Bracket is made by skater on outside foot; for the second three and bracket the skaters have changed rôles.]

13. $\left\{\begin{array}{l}\text{Forward three}\\ \text{Bracket}\end{array}\right\}$ *and* O F Mohawk, *and* forward. [The bracket is made by skater on outside foot.]

14. Forward Mohawk, back inside Q, I F Mohawk, *and* I F reverse Q.

15. *Left-hand skater.* Forward, *and* forward. . . . *and* forward, *and* once back, *and* forward.

    Right-hand skater. Forward, *and* once back, *and* forward, *and* forward, *and* forward . . .

    [During the "*once back*," the skater on the O B passes across the other, and the skaters change sides. While one skater does "once back, *and* forward" the other merely continues on an O F edge.]

Face-to-face scuds

In face-to-face scuds, one skater is on a forward, the other on a back, edge. These cannot be extemporised with the same ease as side-by-side scuds, since the skaters are not simultaneously skating the same movement.

Selected répertoire of face-to-face scuds

The following is a useful selection of scuds of this class: [N.B.—A. starts on a forward, B. on a back edge. The letters R and L, after the movement, indicate which foot the skater commences with, whether right or left.]

1. A. Forward three, *and* back (R).

    B. Back, *and* forward three (L).

    [This movement does not alternate.]

2. A. Forward three, *and* back, *and* back (R).

    B. Back, *and* forward, *and* forward three (L).

    [This is known as the "Mercury Scud."]

3. A. Forward two turns, *and* forward, *and* forward (R).

    B. Back two turns, *and* back, *and* back (L).

4. A. Forward Q (R).

    B. Reverse Q. [An I B serpentine is skated by the right foot, before beginning the reverse Q on the left.]

5. A. Forward Q, *and* back, *and* back (R).

   B. Back, *and* I F, *and* forward Q (R).

   [B.'s back edge is held till A.'s serpentine is finished; B.'s I F edge coinciding with the back edge after the A turn of the Q skated by A.]

6. A. Forward Q, *and* back Q, *and* O F (R).

   B. Back Q, *and* forward Q, *and* O B (L).

7. A. Forward three, *and* back three, *and* forward (R).

   B. Back three, *and* forward three, *and* back (L).

8. A. I F bracket, *and* bracket, *and* I F (R).

   B. I B bracket, *and* O F bracket, *and* I B (L).

9. A. Forward rocker, *and* back rocker, *and* O F (R).

   B. Back rocker, *and* forward rocker, *and* O B (L).

10. A. I F three, *and* O B three, *and* I F (R).

    B. Back three, *and* I F three, *and* O B (R).

11. A. Forward three, *and* I B three, *and* O F Choctaw, *and* I B three (R).

    B. I B three, *and* forward three, *and* I B, *and* I B, *and* forward three (R).

    [During the last part of the Choctaw, both skaters being on the I B edge, A. executes a pass behind B.]

12. A. Forward counter, *and* back counter, *and* O F (R).

    B. Back counter, *and* forward counter, *and* O B (L).

13. A. Mohawk, change, *and* I F, change (R).

B. I B, *and* I F, change Mohawk, back change (R).

[Which ever is skating the back edge of the Mohawk runs behind the other before changing the edge. When the figure commences on the right foot, A. passes to the left of B., and *vice-versâ*.

In all the above scuds, both side-by-side and face-to-face, it is possible for one of the skaters to reverse all the edges by starting on the other foot.

Method of skating side-by-side scuds on different feet

In side-by-side scuds thus skated, the skaters are both on the outside, or both on the inside foot, the one therefore being an outside, the other on an inside, edge.

The rules for precedence given above hold good in this style of hand-in-hand skating, as will be seen from the following illustration:

Suppose the call to be I F three, and the right-hand skater starts on the I F edge on the right foot, and makes an A turn. The left-hand skater in order to travel on a different edge, on the same curve as his partner, must start on the O F edge of the left foot, and make a C turn. Now, according to the rules laid down, whether the left-hand skater is about to make a C turn on the left foot, or an A turn on the right, he must equally follow in the other's tracks. Each skater therefore has merely to follow the rule for the actual edge and subsequent turn he proposes skating, without thinking of what he would have to do were he travelling on the same edge and foot as his partner, since the difference of edge, involving as it does a change of foot, prevents any necessity for altering his *rôle*.

Scuds may be skated of a more complex nature than those here given, by a combination of the various styles, but as the subject is merely touched on here with a view to the possible introduction of hand-in-hand skating in combined movements to a centre, those who wish to make a special study of this branch of the art are referred to the book by N. G. Thompson and L. Cannan ("Hand-in-hand Figure Skating," Longmans, Green, and Co.).[57]

Scuds as dance steps

All scuds may be used as dance steps by giving a fixed value to each part of the movement, so as to skate in rhythm, keeping time with the music.

The number of possible dance steps is therefore practically inexhaustible, especially as various two-footed movements may be pressed into the service.

---

[57] Published in 1896.

Appendix II. Care of rinks

All those who regard skating seriously are keenly alive to the necessity of good ice, and wherever rinks are properly managed, provided there be sufficient frost, a good surface for skating can generally be secured in the first instance.[58]

But many persons, who gladly avail themselves of good ice when there, do not sufficiently realise that it depends to a great extent on themselves whether the surface be *preserved* in a satisfactory state, or whether it become a hideous spectacle covered with blotches and pitted with holes.

Without the co-operation of skaters the rink maker cannot preserve the ice in its original pure state, which is only possible by *scrupulous cleanliness*.

Particles of dirt, or any foreign substance, such as matches, cigarette ends, cigar ashes, and the like, when dropped about on a rink, speedily eat their way into the ice, or corrode the surface.

The least observant can hardly have failed to notice what happens when a stray leaf has fluttered on to the ice. Unless at once removed, it soon becomes firmly embedded, and sinks deeper and deeper, this process of destruction only ceasing when every particle of the foreign substance which caused the mischief has been removed.

The damage, it is true, may be more or less satisfactorily repaired, but this involves considerable labour, and the spot operated on always remains a blemish, which may give trouble later on.

---

[58]This seems particularly important in view of the need for extremely large ice surfaces before indoor ice rinks and ice-resurfacing machines became common.

A moment's reflection will convince anyone that a similar process must take place whatever foreign substance finds its way onto the ice, resulting in its disfigurement by unsightly blotches and dangerous holes. Such a condition is abhorrent to all true skaters, who should have the same solicitude for the surface of their rink as a fair maid for her complexion.

On most well-kept rinks certain rules are posted up, for the guidance of those unacquainted with the treatment of ice, which some whose skating education is still in an elementary state, are at times apt to regard as interference with the liberty of the subject.

A little experience, however, teaches them that such regulations are in the interests of all, and their utility is so fully recognized by more mature skaters, that they would scrupulously act up to them were no restrictions of the sort imposed. Such notes are generally to the effect that—

Skaters are requested not to come on to the rink, except with skates on (since otherwise they might convey with them particles of mud and dirt).

Skaters are requested not to drop matches, cigarette ends, ashes, &c., on the rink (since these at into the ice and produce holes), &c., &c.

That such restrictions are absolutely necessary is self-evident to those who understand the nature of ice, and the wanton damage caused by some skaters is, for the most part, the result of thoughtlessness or ignorance.

As regards smoking, an absolute prohibition to do so while actually skating would no doubt be best for the rink; but, in default of this, every care should be taken not to drop ashes on the ice, while throwing about matches and cigarette ends should, of course, be out of the question.

Where all those who use a rink combine to keep the

surface *perfectly clean*, and free from all foreign substances whatsoever, the task of the rink maker is considerably lightened, and skaters are able to enjoy their sport under the most favourable conditions.

Let those, then, who are little versed in the nature of ice take the above to heart, and on the rink, as elsewhere, bear in mind that "*Cleanliness is next to godliness!*"

Also available from
Skating History Press
Publishing new editions of historic books about skating.

A Treatise on Skating
R. Jones
First published in 1772, this is the oldest surviving book about ice skating. This edition includes the full text of the original work, the sheet music for "The Skater's March," and W. E. Cormack's 1855 revisions, plus a new introduction and notes.

98+iv pages, illustrated

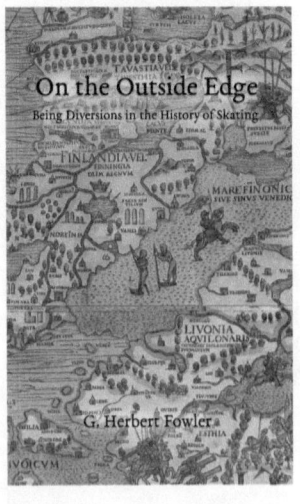

On the Outside Edge
G. Herbert Fowler
A clever and insightful history of skating, this book traces the development of figure skating through the late nineteenth century. This edition—the first since 1897—uses the results of current scholarship to bring Fowler's work up to date.

145+iv pages, illustrated

Frostiana

A souvenir of the last great Frost Fair, *Frostiana* has a reputation for having been printed on the frozen Thames. It contains numerous amusing anecdotes about winter events and activities. This edition includes a new introduction and period illustrations.

165+vi pages, illustrated

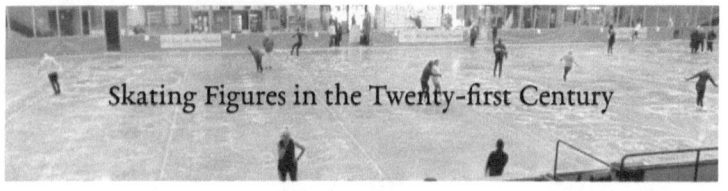

Yes, you can still skate figures!

Even if your rink doesn't offer patch sessions any more, you can still practice, test, and compete compulsory figures and even special figures. This free online resource guide has all the information you need to get started or continue. Whether you're a beginner wondering what figures are or a seasoned skater looking for a new pair of patch skates, you'll find what you need here.

http://www.skatinghistorypress.com/

www.ingramcontent.com/pod-product-compliance
Lightning Source LLC
Chambersburg PA
CBHW030052100526
44591CB00008B/112